Reincarnation - *The Gospel Truth*

Reincarnation - *The Gospel Truth*

by

Martha Knobloch

Printed in the United States of America
ISBN 0-914903-51-9

Destiny Image Publishers
P.O. Box 351
Shippensburg, PA 17257

Contents

CHAPTER	PAGE
Preface	
Scriptural References, Abbreviations	
1. Beginnings, Rationale	1
2. Rebirth, Universal Fatherhood of God	11
3. Animal Souls? Spirit, Soul, Body	17
4. Ecology — Reusable Souls?	21
5. Karma, Justice, Personal God	25
6. Natural, Carnal, Spiritual	35
7. God's Love and/or Justice (Judgment Day, Resurrection)	45
8. Second Chance? Death, Spiritual	55
9. Death, Physical	67
10. Origen and Justinian	77
11. Elijah and John the Baptist: Jacob and Esau	81
12. Remembered Lives, Deja vu, Demons	93
13. Satan, Witchcraft	115
14. Edgar Cayce	139
15. More Cayce	149
16. Human Reasoning — Ruth Montgomery	163
17. More Human Reasoning — Head and Cranston	171
18. Theosophy	179
19. Shirley MacLaine and Company	187
20. Rainbows and Swastikas	195
21. Personal Testimony — The Way Out	205
Notes	213

About the illustration: As in life, Jewish and Christian symbols are prominent but may be hard to discern. Central and visible through both is Jesus of Nazareth, a Jew. At upper left is the many-roomed dream house which led the author into belief in reincarnation, as described in the preface. In a clockwise direction; a figure beckons by a knobless door. A monkey signifies questions of evolution, transmigration and Eastern religions. The blocks of Stonehenge symbolize other ancient beliefs. At the lower left we see the tightrope walker over swirling waters as mentioned in the text. Continuing clockwise; a chair indicates meditation or prayer, a lamp nearby sheds light. Encompassing all, the border represents stone tablets of scripture. Other symbolism is there for the finding.

Scriptural References, Abbreviations

All scripture references are from the New Scofield Reference Bible, Authorized King James Version (NY: Oxford University Press, 1967), unless otherwise noted.

NAS: New American Standard Bible New Testament, Text Edition, (Carol Stream, IL: Creation House, 1960, 1972).

LB: The Living Bible, (Wheaton, IL: Tyndale House, Christianity Today Edition, 1971).

ANT: The Amplified New Testament, (La Habra, CA: The Lockman Foundation, 1958).

TEV: The New Testament in Today's English Version, *Good News for Modern Man*, (NY: Pocket Books), 1969, or *Good News Bible*, Today's English Version, (NY: American Bible Society, 1966, 1971, 1976).

RSV: Revised Standard Version, Harper Study Bible, (Grand Rapids, MI: Zondervan, 1952, 1985).

NEB: The New English Bible New Testament, (Oxford University Press, Cambridge University Press, 1961).

Words within references in bold type are author's emphasis.

Preface

In my dream, I was in a strangely familiar house. It was unlike any place I have ever lived, yet I knew it was my house. As I went through, I kept finding rooms I had forgotten were there. I recognized each furnishing in each room and marveled that I could have let these memories slip away.

This dream, vivid and recurring, was the beginning of my study into the subject of reincarnation.

Eventually, I saw reincarnation as a lovely completion of my Christian faith; then came an ordinary miracle.

The author wishes to thank Lauren Nethery for her typing and production assistance, Sherry Heller for the illustration, and Norman Edgerly for the line drawing. Photo by Sherry Heller. This is also to express appreciation to the many people who have helped in a myriad of ways. You know who you are!

This work is dedicated with love
to those who seek to combine
reincarnation with Christianity.

ONE

Beginnings, Rationale

REINCARNATION	Rebirth of a human soul into a new human body.
TRANSMIGRATION	Rebirth of any soul into a different life form.
KARMA	Consequence of a past life seen in the present.
OCCULT	Supernatural things unrevealed, secret.
CHRISTIAN	Any person who has experienced a new birth of the Spirit as Jesus Christ taught.
GRACE	God's unmerited favor.
REDEEM	To buy back out of slavery.
RESURRECTION	Life restored to a dead body.
GOSPEL	The good news.

Disaster can begin in such innocent ways! Take for instance, a fuzzy definition of terms. No one had ever defined for me the meaning of the word "Christian," so as I grew up in America, a "Christian nation," it seemed to me that anyone not a Jew was automatically a Christian. Eastern religions had nothing to do with me or anyone I knew. Within the assumption that I was a Christian lay the seeds of disaster. They sprouted as I began to think of myself as a "good Christian" because of natural religious and moral inclinations. Daily I watered those disastrous sprouts by trying to be "better" than other people, and hoping good deeds outweighed the bad. What brought it to a head was the dream of a many-roomed house described in the preface.

That curious dream became so frequent and insistent that it couldn't be ignored. I didn't understand it, but I began to think that my subconscious mind was trying to tell me something.

Then, unexpectedly, I discovered a book about Edgar Cayce. While in a trance, Cayce would diagnose and prescribe odd cures for medical disorders. Although medically untrained, his accuracy seemed phenomenal. Edgar Cayce was a Bible reader, a Sunday School teacher who talked about Jesus and claimed his own strange powers were gifts from God. I wanted to believe his every word. Cayce also did dream interpretations, one of which was especially interesting to me. He taught that in dreams, a house represents a soul, and the rooms are different lives lived by that soul. This was a whole new idea to me, but if it were true, it would explain why everything in my dream house was so familiar.

Reincarnation? I knew that the Christian church does not teach it, so I was cautious. Was it in the Bible? Bible reading had been an important part of my religious life, but most of it was unclear to me. Perhaps I had simply missed reincarnation. Edgar Cayce even taught about the Bible and it seemed that his mystical powers confirmed his knowledge.

I yearned to know the truth, one way or the other. I began to read everything I could find on reincarnation. It was hard to keep an open mind, because it seemed that every author then writing about reincarnation believed in it. In my readings, authors frequently quoted Bible passages which they claimed proved their beliefs. More and more, I began to accept their theories. It didn't seem fair to bother my busy pastor with my questions, so I didn't ask him. Seeking answers, I joined a Sunday school class studying comparative religions and learned what Hindus and others believe about reincarnation. Somehow, I still did not realize that I did not understand Christianity.

After one full year of study, I mistakenly concluded that reincarnation was true, for the following reasons:

* I misunderstood the Biblical term "born again."

* I believed in the "universal fatherhood of God."

* I learned that reincarnationists do not necessarily accept transmigration. (I could not believe that human souls proceed from or to lower life forms.)

* I recognized the economy of nature and applied this rule to human souls.

* I thought karma provided a rationale for justice in the world.

* My acceptance of reincarnation seemed natural, reasonable, and harmless.

* I felt a deep desire to believe in a God of total love and total fairness.

* The Bible, as I understood it, did not seem to teach against reincarnation.

* I ignored spiritual death and refused to acknowledge fear of physical death.

* I accepted what I read about Origen and Justinian.

* I interpreted Christ's assertion of Elijah's coming again as support for reincarnation.

* I had heard of and personally experienced deja vu, significant dreams and bits of "remembered" lives.
* I was influenced by Edgar Cayce's intermingling of Christianity and reincarnation.
* I failed to see that belief in reincarnation opened for me the door to Satan's occult kingdom.
* I did not recognize the progressive dangers of being outside Biblical guidelines.
* Certain writers and philosophies teaching reincarnation seemed intelligent and logical.

Because of my misunderstandings, I became a reincarnationist. No one else I knew believed in reincarnation. However, I was careful not to advocate this belief to anyone since a gnawing uncertainty remained deep inside. It didn't seem important whether others believed in reincarnation or not. I rationalized that they simply had not reached my "level of understanding" and may be enlightened in their next life.

I noted with satisfaction that as soon as I accepted reincarnation, my dream vanished. It seemed that my "subconscious mind" was now at ease.

For the next five years, despite active church involvement, I believed that each soul progresses through a series of human lives until finally becoming worthy of dwelling with God forever. The arrogance of that escaped me.

Little did I know that my disaster was well under way. As I became more deeply convinced of reincarnation, I was completely oblivious to what was really happening. Ever so slowly, imperceptibly, I floated down into a pit. I began to be uncharacteristically depressed. I barely noticed that what little faith I had in God had dwindled away. My feeble attempts at prayer ended without regret. Instead of trying to eliminate my faults, I daydreamed about what "karma" had caused them. When I tried to do what was right, it was for the wrong reasons.

Belief in reincarnation did not make me a better person, nor did it provide strength for everyday living. A fatalistic attitude permeated my thinking and all of life became trivial. I stopped all Bible reading.

Eventually, the depression became so bad that I began to seriously consider suicide. I wondered about my sanity because outwardly there was absolutely no reason for either depression or suicide.

In desperation I tried "relaxation therapy" (hypnosis), and was very relieved when the depression lifted somewhat. I normally enjoy people, but at this point I became more and more withdrawn. My thoughts centered increasingly upon myself, and what my past and future lives might be, and with whom. The depression recurred, worse than before.

There's no telling where all this might have led if God had not intervened. A small group in my church had planned a one day retreat and a friend insisted on taking me. A special quality emanated from the woman speaker and I dimly recognized something in her which was good. Somehow, she was different. I have no idea what she said, but at one point, she asked that we separate and sit alone to pray. Scattered throughout the house and grounds, others were praying, but not me. I just couldn't. In my misery, I at last recognized how far I had removed myself from God.

Alone later, I finally managed a one word prayer. On my knees with hands upraised and tears streaming, I simply said, "Help!" This cry came from the depths of me, and God heard.

Just as I had floated down into the pit, now by the grace of God I began to be slowly lifted out.

Whatever disaster had awaited me in the pit below, ever so gradually it became more distant as God continued to draw me up and out. The Bible began to interest me again slightly, and once in a while a small prayer was in my heart. The daydreaming decreased. What was happening in the here-and-now became more interesting. I began to face up to my faults rather than alibi them away. Fears of suicide and madness subsided. Even the chair I had used for "relaxation therapy" was sent out of the house for repairs, and I couldn't get comfortable anywhere else. God had every detail firmly in hand.

As I said in the beginning, I had always believed myself to be a Christian, and the Lord was very patient in teaching me the truth. It was several months before I understood what that simple one word prayer had done. Three subtle changes were taking place in my life: (1) the depression gradually lifted, (2) a deep quiet peace began to permeate me, and (3) the obsession with self faded as God and others became more important to me.

Seven months later, I had a telephone conversation with a cousin, an artist who understands spiritual matters. He told me that he was praying for a relative of ours to be saved. His attitude struck me as "holier-than-thou," and I was annoyed. I said, "Well, she believes in Jesus. Isn't she saved?" With great kindness and love, he answered, "No, Martha. You know the picture of Jesus standing at the door and knocking?" I knew the one he meant. "It's not particularly good art, but it is scriptural," he explained.

"What do you mean?"

"There's no doorknob on the outside."

"So?"

"So it can't be opened from the outside. Jesus will enter our hearts only when we open from the inside and invite him in. He's such a gentleman, he'll never force himself on anyone who doesn't invite him to come in. That picture illustrates Revelation 3:20. Jesus says, 'Behold, I stand at the door and knock; if any man hear my voice, and open the door, I will come in to him.' "

Suddenly, it seemed that someone had switched on a floodlight in my head. After all the years of darkness, I finally understood!

Astonishment overwhelmed me as I saw for the first time ever what it means to be "born again!" I understood at last that having Jesus' Holy Spirit dwelling in us brings the new birth, and that he enters only when specifically invited. I saw in a flash how mistaken I had been all my life, as I had assumed that because I **intellectually** believed in Jesus, I was a Christian. I saw that a Christian is one who has Jesus inside and who believes in him as their own personal Lord and Savior.

Immediately after this telephone conversation, I chose a record of "music to think by," and turned on the stereo, switching it to "phono." I watched amazed as the phonograph worked, but the radio sounded instead! It never did **that** before (or since)! There was a preacher talking; it was the tail-end of a sermon. He said, "Listen! Christian! Don't think you are saved just because you believe in Jesus. You must **ASK** him to come into your heart and life!"

I couldn't believe this had actually happened. For almost forty years, I had wandered in the wilderness, not understanding. Now, twice in ten minutes, God had told me the one thing I really needed to know.

My life since that day has been one of many miracles. One "coincidence" after another, by the hundreds, has brought me nearer the Savior. It's a day-by-day excitement that nothing else can touch when one **walks** and **talks** with and **is** a child of the King of Kings!

As Jesus says in the third chapter of the Gospel of John: "Ye must be born again." I had memorized it, but had not understood its meaning. Suddenly, I was reborn in the same body! With rebirth, as befits any creature just born, a new plane of existence begins and old things are passed away (2 Corinthians 5:17). As a new creature, I was given new understanding as well as a new nature.

I reasoned that a Supreme Being, if one existed, must have others over which to be supreme. How could God be God without communicating his existence to us? And he did! He certainly had found a way to reach me, and I saw nature and the Bible as further means of communication. A reading of the first chapter of the Gospel of John revealed to me that Jesus is so much God's communication to us that he is actually called "the Word." "In the beginning was the Word, and the Word was with God, and the Word was God (John 1:1)." Further in the same chapter, we find "...and the Word was made flesh and dwelt among us (John 1:14)." The rest of the gospel identifies "the Word" as Jesus Christ, and John and others as his eyewitnesses.

After spiritual rebirth, my search for truth became so intense that I was willing even to seriously study teachings opposing reincarnation. I began to see truths in the Bible which I could not see before.

I finally realized that, as my pride had urged me to seek for "deeper" truths, my foolishness had blinded me to **obvious** truth. The falsehood of reincarnation had shut out God's truth. It was as if I had been trying to diaper an unborn baby; but first things simply must be first. Truth cannot be built on a false foundation.

I once attended a meeting where many sweet and well-meaning people, who were there to learn, were actually sharing their ignorance instead. The consensus was: "Figure out what a scripture means for yourself. That's what is true for you." While it may be a fact that two people can read the same verse and learn entirely different lessons, basic Bible truths are true for all people. Since any one verse can be misunderstood, it's vital to compare each verse to others. The Bible always proves itself. "No prophecy of the scripture is of any private interpretation (2 Peter 1:20)."

My spiritual rebirth made a tremendous difference in my understanding and attitude toward the scriptures. The Bible teaches that the believer is indwelt by the Holy Spirit, and that the same Holy Spirit is the actual Author of the Book. "For no prophecy was ever made by an act of human will, but men moved by the Holy Spirit spoke from God (2 Peter 1:21 NAS)."

Like millions of other people I can testify that, after spiritual rebirth, the Bible "opens up" and comes alive as never before. This vast difference cannot be overstated.

The spirit within me knows that the Bible is true. Jesus prayed for believers, "Sanctify them through thy truth: thy word is truth (John 17:17)." I asked the Lord to help in areas of unbelief, and he did. I claimed the promise of James 1:5 (NAS): "If any of you lacks wisdom, let him ask of God, who gives to all men generously and without reproach, and it will be given to him." It took a few months, but as the Holy Spirit within me grew, I eventually came to know that the Bible is pure and given indeed by inspiration of God (2 Timothy 3:16).

Someone may say, "Suppose something in the Bible were proved to be wrong. Wouldn't this end your faith?" My answer is, "No!". While the Christian's faith is constantly built up by the truths of the Bible, it is not the object of our worship. We worship the true and living God, and thanks to his grace alone, have a personal relationship with him. Most reverently, I can say that God is my close and well-known friend, as well as my king. My trust is in him because I know him.

Many volumes have been written to show the literal and total truth of the Bible. To name a few, I recommend: *Evidence That Demands a Verdict*[1], *Know Why You Believe*[2], *None of These Diseases*[3], *The Tabernacle*[4], and *Questions New Christians Ask*[5].

The more I was willing to study the Bible in context, and as a unit (rather than isolated verses), the more its wisdom and the validity of its teachings took shape. I learned that the plainest meaning is primary. One by one, each reason I had for clinging to belief in reincarnation crumbled away; each was replaced by truth far more satisfying. In the following chapters, I will deal with each one of these erroneous opinions and the life-giving truth which took its place.

TWO

Rebirth, Universal Fatherhood of God

I have mentioned a few of the things the rebirth did for me, but I would like to share with you what it actually is. Jesus Christ taught that the new birth is spiritual rather than physical. He said, "It is the spirit that giveth life; the flesh profiteth nothing (John 6:63)." If, then, the flesh profits nothing, how many physical lives would we need to be acceptable to God? All multiples of zero equal zero. It follows that an infinite number of physical lives would still equal nothing. A spiritual rebirth is the requirement. But such confusion there is about this!

The contemporaries of Jesus were no different from us in this respect. Nicodemus, an extremely religious man, leader of religious men, came to Jesus to learn. "Sir," he said, "we all know that God has sent you to teach us. Your miracles are proof enough of this."

Jesus replied, "With all the earnestness I possess I tell you this: Unless you are born again, you can never get into the Kingdom of God."

"Born again!" exclaimed Nicodemus. "What do you mean? How can an old man go back into his mother's womb and be born again?" Jesus replied,

> What I am telling you so earnestly is this: Unless one is born of water and the Spirit, he cannot enter the Kingdom of God. Men can only reproduce human life, but the Holy Spirit gives new life from heaven; so don't be surprised at my statement that you must be born again! Just as you can hear the wind but can't tell where it comes from or where it will go next, so it is with the Spirit. We do not know on whom he will next bestow this life from heaven (John 3:2-8 LB).

Nicodemus was called a respected teacher by Jesus. He did not even think of reincarnation, but just asked how an old man could go back to his mother's womb. He knew "born again" did not mean physical rebirth and was utterly bewildered. Jesus clearly meant a spiritual rebirth.

A little further in this conversation, Jesus explained to Nicodemus exactly how to obtain eternal life through the rebirth:

> For God so loved the world that he gave his only begotten Son, that whosoever believeth in him should not perish, but have everlasting life (John 3:16).

Many years later, Peter told Christians:

> For you have a new life. It was not passed on to you from your parents, for the life they gave you will fade away. This new one will last forever, for it comes from Christ, God's ever-living Message to men (1 Peter 1:23 LB).

Jesus said, "I am the way, the truth, and the life; no man cometh unto the Father, but by me (John 14:6)." It is belief in him which gives the new life. Yet a sloppy, half-hearted belief will not do.

The story is told of a tightrope walker who proved to a large crowd that he was able to walk a tightrope across the top of roaring Niagara Falls. They had great confidence that he could do it again. But when he asked who would trust him enough to let him carry them on his back, no one volunteered. They believed, but not that much! Anyone who would do that would have to rely totally on him. This kind of total reliance is a perfect picture of the word "believer." It is belief in Jesus — total reliance — which gives new life. Further, this total reliance demands a decision — a definite point of no return. Shall I volunteer to ride the tight rope walker's back or not? If I choose to get on, there's no changing my mind. Shall I rely completely on Jesus as he invites me to? The choice is mine. Not to choose him is to choose the false hope of my own works.

We are all children of God!

This is a statement which I have heard often and made often myself. Many people believe it, and they feel that since we are all God's children we will all eventually be taken into his presence, one way or another.

Yet the Bible teaches that we are not all God's children; that we will NOT all be taken to heaven by virtue of the fact that God created us.

It is true that God created everything and everyone. It is true that he sent his Son to die for us all, because he loves the **world** (all of us). It is true that he is not willing that **any** of us should perish. But these things do NOT make us his children, according to God's word.

We are given the power to **become** children of God by receiving God's Son.

> But to all who received him, he gave the right to **become** children of God. All they needed to do was trust him to save them. All those who believe this are reborn! — not a physical rebirth resulting from human passion or plan —but from the will of God (John 1:12,13 LB).

Like all the great doctrines of the word of God, this concept is taught in the Bible in many different places with different phraseology to avoid heretical twisting of verses by taking them out of context.

Whether reading a newspaper or the Bible, the reader must know to whom a quote is addressed in order to understand the quotation properly. For example, in a following passage, Jesus speaks to the Pharisees and says that they are of their father, the devil. No one claims that Jesus meant this for everyone who reads it. Yet, many people take Bible statements that we are God's children and try to make them apply to everyone! For this reason, addressees are noted in the following quotes. Are we all children of God? See for yourself!

John 8:38,41,44-47 (The Pharisees, religious leaders, argue with Jesus).

Jesus says,

> I speak that which I have seen with **my** Father, and ye do that which ye have seen with **your** father. Ye do the deeds of your father. Then said they to him, we are not born of fornication; we have one Father, even God. Jesus said unto them, If God were your Father, ye would love me; for I proceeded forth and came from God; neither came I of myself, but he sent me. Ye are of **your father, the devil,** and the lusts of your father ye will do. He was a murderer from the beginning, and abode not in the truth, because there is no truth in him. When he speaketh a lie, he speaketh of his own; for he is a liar, and the father of it. And because I tell you the truth, ye believe me not. Which of you convicteth me of sin? And if I say the truth, why do ye not believe me? He that is of God heareth God's word; ye, therefore, hear them not, because **ye are not of God.**

1 John 5:18-21 LB (St. John the Beloved to believers).

> No one who has become a part of God's family makes a practice of sinning, for Christ, God's Son, holds him securely and the devil cannot get his hands on him. We know that we are the children of God and that all the rest of the world around us is under Satan's power and control. And we know Christ, God's Son, has come to help us understand and find the true God. And now we are in God because we are in Jesus Christ his Son, who is the only true God; and he is eternal Life. Dear children, keep away from anything that might take God's place in your hearts.

In the charming story of Pinocchio, the carver wanted a son so badly that he created a boy puppet. But he was unable to give him life. The created thing was his creation, but not his son. God also created each of us, and is able to give life. Not wanting puppets, he gave us free will, and an opportunity to choose spiritual life, or to reject it. If we choose his way, he gives us true life, and we become, not the created thing, but his own child. Ye must be born again!

THREE

Animal Souls? Spirit, Soul, Body.

What do you think? Do animals have souls or not? Everyone knows of the Hindu worship of sacred cows and other kinds of reverence for any form of life. We can all tell stories of pets or wild animals with very special qualities. Legend has it that Buddha, in an early life as a rabbit, threw himself in the fire to prevent someone's starvation.

Usually, the idea that a soul can move from a lower animal form to a higher form or vice versa is called transmigration. Some reincarnationists accept this theory. I simply never did. I knew that God said in Genesis 1, "Let us make man in our image, after our likeness." In the same verse, God gave man dominion over all creatures. Many times, the Bible states that the creatures all reproduced "after their own kind."

Some transmigrationists will tell you that apes and chimps are those souls nearly ready to advance to human form. This idea is contradicted over and over in God's word.

With thought, we can see that there is no real need to go beneath the human race for a wide range of experiences in order to reach "soul readiness."

Mr. Dean Barton, a layman devoted to Christ, makes the following interesting statement on this topic:

> In order to function on this planet, both humans and animals need physical bodies which provide the five senses normally needed to survive: taste, touch, sight, smell and hearing. But we also have emotions, will and intellect which emanate, not from the body, but from the soul. Therefore, the mind and personality are of the soul, not physical. We know that animals have emotions, intelligence and personalities of their own. By this definition then, both people and animals have body and soul. As far as we can tell, animals do not have the potential to become spiritual beings as well, but we do.[1]

It should be understood that there is a difference between soul and spirit. Trying to understand spiritual matters through the efforts of the soul is as hopeless and frustrating as trying to catch a jar full of wind. The difference between soul and spirit is described especially well by Watchman Nee. In part, he says:

> The Word of God does not divide man into the two parts of soul and body. It treats man, rather, as tripartite —spirit, soul and body. 1 Thessalonians 5:23 reads, 'May the God of peace himself sanctify you wholly; and may your spirit and soul and body be kept sound and blameless at the coming of our Lord Jesus Christ....'
>
> Other portions of the Scriptures make this same differentiation between spirit and soul. For the Word of God is living and active, sharper than any two-edged sword, piercing to the division of soul and spirit, of joints

> and marrow, and discerning the thoughts and intentions of the heart (Hebrews 4:12). The writer of this verse divides man's non-corporal elements into two parts, "soul and spirit." ...It follows that since soul and spirit can be divided, they must be different in nature. It is thus evident that man is a composite of three parts....
>
> To repeat, the soul is the site of personality. The will, intellect and emotions of man are there. As the spirit is used to communicate with the spiritual world and the body with the natural world, so the soul stands between and exercises its power to discern and decide whether the spiritual or the natural world should reign.[2]

I had always assumed that soul and spirit were the same, but that is not so. The soul is that part of us which consists of emotion, will and intellect. The spirit of man is that which is capable of awareness of, and communication with, God. This is why we cannot perceive God by the use of intellect, emotion or will. That which is God (a Spirit) can only be perceived by the spirit, not the soul (See Hebrews 4:12).

> But the natural man receiveth not the things of the Spirit of God; for they are foolishness unto him, neither can he know them, because they are spiritually discerned (1 Corinthians 2:14).

Man's spiritual linkage to God was blocked when sin entered. Adam could not pass on to his descendants that which he did not possess. Each one of us must move to renew that link for ourselves. Our spirit is the only "ear" we have to hear God.

So if you believe that your pet has a soul, you're right. It has intellect, emotion, and will. But it lacks the ability to understand spiritual matters. It does not have the potential to trust in Christ as human beings do. As a wise little child put it, "Mommy, people can pray, but animals can't."

The Bible teaches that any human being who accepts Jesus Christ as their own Lord and Savior is spiritually born and shall live eternally in heaven; that their personality shall be intact, their body perfect and their joy complete. This is surely a far better hope than any other — and based on God's word, not man's.

Christ died for all — that's history.

Christ died for me — that's salvation!

This personal relationship to Christ cannot be attained by use of will, emotion or intellect. It is spiritual. A baby can't use his intellect, emotion or will to understand his parent's love to him. He just accepts it. In the same simple way, we must accept the love God offers us. Jesus said, "Except ye be converted, and become as little children, ye shall not enter into the kingdom of heaven (Matthew 18:3)."

FOUR

Ecology — Reusable Souls?

As I gazed out the window, I noticed an apple leaf fall and realized that the leaf would eventually become soil and be used again and again. Would it ever disappear completely? No; as matter, the atoms would have to take some form or other. When I applied this reasoning to reincarnation, it seemed to me that the recycling process scored on the side of reincarnation. Nothing is wasted in nature. Would God, who had formed such a perfect plan in nature, allow souls to be wasted by sending any to Hell? Wouldn't they be recycled until worthy of his presence?

This sounds logical, but it is faulty logic and uses an invalid argument of reasoning by analogy. The atoms of that leaf were matter — material, if you like. But the soul, as any scientist would agree, is not physical material.

Once again, I had conveniently overlooked scripture. In Genesis 1:26 God said, "Let us make man in our image," a very special case! Of all the things God created, only man was in his image.

In Genesis 2:7, the Bible says, "And the Lord God formed man of the dust of the ground, and breathed into his nostrils the breath of life; and man became a living soul." Not even Michelangelo's magnificent rendering of God's finger reaching out to Adam's catches the grandeur of this! What a drama! There was man's body, formed and lifeless, until the all-holy, perfect and everlasting God breathed his **own** breath into the nostrils to give life!

When do souls originate? In Adam's case, only after God breathed into his nostrils. The theory of reincarnation rests on the supposition that the soul is immortal. Immortal means no beginning, no ending, exempt from death. The Bible teaches that God is the only immortal being, and that all else is created by him. Reincarnation claims that the soul has always existed and always will. The Bible says that each soul is given life and breath by God's gift and that it continues to exist by his grace alone. For us to take a life is sin because it usurps God's role.

Surely only God knows the precise moment when a soul is created. But we do know that each person with life is special and precious to him. His word promises that eventually we will fully understand.

> Now all that I know is hazy and blurred, but then I will see everything clearly, just as clearly as God sees into my heart right now (1 Corinthians 13:12 LB).

Even though we now cannot understand completely, we do have promises of God to stand on — this tests our faith. For God honors faith above sight and above reason. Abraham, against reason, believed God's promise that he and his wife would become parents at last in their old age. Beyond that, he trusted the promise that through that child, he, Abraham, would become the father of many nations. Look at Romans 4:3. "Abraham **believed God,** and it was counted unto him for righteousness!"

God honors faith above sight and above reason. When we see God, it will be too late to accept him by faith.

> For we shall all stand before the judgment seat of Christ. As it is written, 'As I live,' saith the Lord, 'every knee shall bow to me, and every tongue shall confess to God.' So, then **every one** of us shall give account of himself to God (Romans 14:10-12). There is nothing wasted!

Jesus even said that every idle word spoken shall be accounted for in the day of judgment (Matthew 12:36). He said, "For whosoever shall give you a cup of water to drink in my name...shall not lose his reward (Mark 9:41)." Nothing wasted! He claimed that the very hairs on our heads are numbered (Matthew 10:30). There is nothing wasted!

Does the economy of God include souls? The question still remains — would God allow souls to be wasted by sending any to condemnation?

Souls which go to hell will go of their own choosing and not because it is God's wish. One verse of the many that tell us this is 2 Peter 3:9. "The Lord...is longsuffering toward us, **not willing that any should perish,** but that all should come to repentance."

Even the souls that are condemned will recognize the justice of their sentence. The fact that they are there in hell will prove God's fairness, thus glorifying him. That would be serving a useful purpose and not a waste at all!

The God of the Bible is the true God. His will is that all should come to eternal life, but he has prepared a place of torment, nevertheless. The god that many of us have imagined in our own minds would not do this, since he is a one-sided god of love alone. The Bible reveals the true God as a god of wrath, angry with sinners all the day long. No, he does not want any souls wasted, precisely because he has gone to so much trouble to provide us a way of salvation. Though it is simple for us to receive it, this salvation was not bought by God at a cheap price. It cost him dearly. Think how we feel when we go to a lot of expense and sacrifice to do something for someone who not only does not appreciate it, but knowingly, totally rejects it! Multiply this feeling by infinity and arrive at God's wrath toward those who reject his son's sacrifice of himself for them.

If we begin with the assumption that God owes us something, we are building on sinking sand. He owes us nothing. He has created and provided us with everything we are and have. We are the clay; he is the potter.

The sayings of Jesus prove that he is wise, not foolish. He came out of love for us because his coming was necessary to provide mankind with the way so that some could be saved. Otherwise, there could be no way. All of us, from birth onward, are marching to hell, and the miracle is that any are redeemed, since all are sinners. The same Bible which says, "The soul that sinneth, it shall die," also says, "Hear, and your soul shall live." Jesus often said, "He that hath ears to hear, let him hear."

Some reincarnationists believe that souls are re-usable based partly on a misunderstanding of Psalm 116:7. This verse says, "Return unto thy rest, O my soul." Here is a perfect example of taking words out of context. In order to understand it, one must read the whole psalm. David is explaining how and why he loves the Lord. I love the Lord because he hears my prayers and answers them. Because he bends down and listens, I will pray as long as I breathe!

> Death stared me in the face — I was frightened and sad. Then I cried, "Lord, save me!" How kind he is! How good he is! So merciful, this God of ours! The Lord protects the simple and the childlike; I was facing death and then he saved me. **Now I can relax.** [Return unto thy rest, O my soul.] For the Lord has done this wonderful miracle for me. He has saved me from death, my eyes from tears, my feet from stumbling. I shall live! Yes, in his presence —here on earth! (Psalm 116:7 LB)

"Return to thy rest, O my soul..." does not mean to die and wait for another body! It does mean now I can relax, for God has answered my prayers.

FIVE

Karma, Justice, Personal God

Karma is believed to be the force for good or evil in the present life as a consequence of behavior during a former life. Some Hindus or Buddhists would hesitate to help a drowning person, for example, lest they interfere with karma: perhaps that person deliberately drowned someone in the last life! Fear of karmic retribution is often carried to extremes and tends to generate a cold and fatalistic attitude. This can cause a callous unconcern for the needs of others, or, on the other side of the coin, enormous confusion when facing simple moral choice. To help, or not to help? How will my decision affect me?

Karma and justice appear to dovetail so beautifully that they're an almost irresistible pair. Do you know an obnoxious person who always gets his own way? Or, do you know someone loving and kind for whom everything goes wrong? That's partly why reincarnation and karma appeal to so many fair-minded people. How perfectly **right** it seems that such as these should finally get comeuppance or reward the next time around! By this reasoning, the racial bigot should be a different race, and the stingy rich man should find out how grinding poverty affects him. The nobody should have a chance at fame; the peon, at monarchy; the homely, at beauty! There are in the world certain men whose daily prayer is "Allah, I thank you that I was not born a woman." Guess what would be in store for them.

All this may sound just fine, but it has several fatal flaws and raises many questions.

These are not flippant questions. If one accepts karma as a law, then one must recognize all results of that law.

If karma exists, why has it not changed human nature by now? History tells us what we were; newspapers tell us what we are.

If an individual is ignorant of prior experiences, how can he possibly learn from them?

If knowledge of former lives would really help, would not God make that information available to us all?

Whom would we suppose supervises all this karmic interaction to get results? (Not God. He says otherwise.)

Are we looking for excuses for our behavior? Or does believing that you had a terrible temper in another life change your responsibility to control it now?

Reincarnation supposes a mystical reason for birth defects. Prenatal care reduces their number. Does "karmic law" make prenatal care immoral?

If the poor and suffering deserve their plight, does the addition of a hospital or a Mother Teresa ministry help or ultimately make things worse? Dare we call such self-sacrificing love evil?

Shouldn't parents add to their "good karma" by feeding many (rats and bugs) rather than few (children)? Reincarnation and karma purists hold all forms of life equal in value. Which tenets are disposable and which are not? Beggar parents in India may break the limbs of their children to increase alms, then abandon them if they are hard to care for. Is this "right" or "wrong?"

Since India has supposedly been the hub of "spiritual awareness" for thousands of years due to reincarnation and karmic teachings, why is the misery there among the world's worst?

If any society erases standards for judging "good or evil," can we not see that anarchy and private chaos are the result?

If a "veil of forgetfulness" exists to protect us from being traumatized by memories of former lives, why tamper with it? And why is such a veil never mentioned in scripture? Why are former lives never mentioned?

What is fair about a "karmic law" which gives no rules and leaves one constantly guessing? Since the Bible makes it clear where God stands on virtually every issue and what he requires of us, isn't that more fair and relevant?

Doesn't the significance of **this** life pale if one believes you can always try again?

Couldn't belief in reincarnation be a desire to "meet oneself" rather than one's Maker?

How can animal souls be so valuable as to foster vegetarianism, yet abortion acceptable since the body of the fetus "does not have a soul yet?" This is a fairly common view. But isn't this an ultimate double standard?

How and why is the world's population increasing if there are no "new" souls being added? If "old" souls are being absorbed back into "being" and all souls are immortal (having no end or beginning), how could there now be souls enough to go around? Christians believe that God gives each new life a unique soul and a unique body; that each of us is totally special and original. This is why so many Christians protest abortion. That unique child forever loses a chance for life, in the Christian view. They cite God's command "Thou shalt not kill." What if they are right?

Thought through, don't reincarnation, karma, abortion, euthanasia, evolution and suicide all cheapen the value of human life? Christ **always** raised the value of human life; so how could any of these dogmas be considered "Christian?"

Are the rich really better people than the poor? Or are their riches punishment rather than reward?

What great humanitarian deeds have been done by Eastern mystics recently adored by certain Westerners? All that comes to mind are tax evasions, gross sexual immorality, enforced marriages and abortions, and a fleet of ninety Rolls-Royces.

Some castes of India believe they must be purified if even touched by the shadow of an "untouchable." How would such a social system affect our lifestyle, if adopted?

If fate and destiny rule all, where is room for the creative, forgiving, redemptive work of God?

Finally, since we are searching for the "gospel truth," what has God said? His word never suggests that man by himself can do anything at all about his sinful condition. Quite the opposite. "There is a way that seemeth right unto a man, but the end thereof are the ways of death (Proverbs 14:12)." Karma would require the working out of wrongs done, as the term "karmic work" tells us. But the scriptures make it abundantly clear that we are saved by grace, "not works, lest any man should boast (Ephesians 2:9)." The Bible plainly shows that we will be punished in hell for our wrongs **or** rewarded in heaven for our faith, according to the destination on our spiritual "ticket." The spiritual ticket of every accountable man, woman and child on earth is marked "hell," since "ALL have sinned, and come short of the glory of God (Romans 3:23)." Only the applied blood of Jesus Christ changes the destination since his is the only way to pay the price.

We like to think of a promise as something pleasant. But, if I tell my child he will be punished, he'd better believe it, because whether he likes it or not, he has received a promise which will be carried out. God has promised us all that there is a hell as well as a heaven. It's immaterial whether we approve.

Notice in Jesus' story of the rich man and Lazarus that neither had a second chance (Luke 16:19-31). This passage is fully discussed in Chapter 8. In Mark 16:16, Christ tells us "He that believeth not shall be damned." He did not say "given another chance." In another statement, Jesus tells us, "And these shall go away into everlasting punishment, but the righteous into life eternal (Matthew 25:46)." Acts 24:15 says flatly that there will be a resurrection of the dead, **both** the just and the unjust (believer and the unbeliever). Jesus Christ repeats the same truth in John 5:29. Clearly, Christian doctrine and the theories of reincarnation and karma are mutually exclusive.

If karma were truth, then there could be no such thing as judgment as described in the Bible. Man would be locked into endless efforts to justify himself. He could never succeed since new "karmic debts" (which God calls sins), would be manifested in each life. His hopes to eventually balance on the positive side of the scales couldn't help even if he achieved it, according to God's word. One who strives to live by the law (good works) must be judged by the law (commandments) and inevitably found wanting (Revelation 20:12,13).

Since ALL have sinned, we can see that an endless number of lives would still not bring us to the required perfection, the holiness needed to face God. To break one law makes you a lawbreaker. To sin one sin makes you a sinner. God's way of actually providing perfection for us is far superior to any other conceivable idea.

Jesus Christ willingly suffered death on the cross to provide that perfection for us. This has been called "The Great Transaction." He became sin for us; we are counted as righteous when we accept Christ.

> ...receive the love he offers you — be reconciled to God.
> For God took the sinless Christ and poured into him our

> sins. Then, in exchange, he poured God's goodness into us! (2 Corinthians 5:20,21 LB).

The idea of karma is certainly vague, pale and hopeless compared to God's way.

Beyond that, Christ's resurrection promises eternal life to those who trust his way. Not an endless cycle of good and bad earthly lives depending on self, but one victorious overcoming life crowned with eternal joy, dependent on God.

If karma were truth, then we could become our own saviors by performing karmic good works. But the Bible teaches that Jesus is the only Savior there is; and that it is by his sacrifice on the cross that we are saved. Hebrews 1:3 says, "When he (Jesus) had **by himself** purged our sins, sat down on the right hand of the Majesty on high."

Since Jesus did this **by himself,** our "good deeds" can do nothing to purge sins of this life or any other! Jesus cried out from the cross, "It is finished! (John 19:30)." What could we possibly add to that which is finished?

It is not karma, but the blood of Jesus which cleanses — "The blood of Jesus Christ, his Son, cleanseth us from all sin (1 John 1:7)."

> Unto him that loveth us, and washed us from our sins in his own blood, and hath made us a kingdom of priests unto God and his Father, to him be glory and dominion forever and ever (Revelation 1:5,6).

Hebrews 9:22 (LB) says, "...without the shedding of blood there is no forgiveness of sins." Medical science tells us that every child's blood is inherited from its father. Since Jesus was conceived by the Holy Spirit (Luke 1:35), his blood is unique and untainted by sin, as he is the Son of God.

> What can wash away my sin? Nothing but the blood of Jesus; What can make me whole again? Nothing but the blood of Jesus. Oh! Precious is the flow That makes me

white as snow; No other fount I know, Nothing but the blood of Jesus.[1]

Jesus said:

> For God so loved (your name) that he gave his only begotten Son, that (your name) believeth in him should not perish, but have everlasting life (John 3:16).

This deep personal love and interest God has in each of us is glorious!

God is not some far away someone, unknowing or unknowable. Some people tend to think of our Creator as a vague "fountain of existence" or "ground of being." However, the Bible shows God as a person; one who urges us to seek and know him (Jeremiah 29:13). He **can** be found, and he **is** knowable. He loves (John 3:16); he hates (Proverbs 6:16); he speaks (Genesis 9:1); he hears (John 9:31); he creates (Genesis 1:27); he heals (Psalm 30:2); he thinks (Psalm 40:17); he remembers (Psalm 105:8); he is a Spirit (John 4:24); he has a will (Matthew 6:10); he has plans (John 10:10); he knows our hearts (Luke 16:15); he cares about **you** personally (1 Peter 5:7). God also has many other characteristics, all of which are traits of living persons.

The question then arises, "If God is there, and is so loving, how could he let such awful things happen?" This is a legitimate question, dealt with here in other chapters, although there is no one simple answer. Like puzzle pieces, many parts fitted together provide the solution, but karma is not part of it.

God knows that the few short years we live on earth will soon be gone, but eternity is what really counts. He will often pour blessing after blessing on a person, hoping that gratitude will win their attention, and that they will turn to him. Sometimes he will allow trouble and turmoil into a life, since that may be the way to save the soul. He will always use the most gentle way possible to break through our rebellion to reach us. Thank God he loves us too much to leave us the way we are! But, since he has given us a free will, we are free to do the most dangerous thing of all — ask God to leave us alone. He wants to bless all people, but those who want him out of their lives will eventually bring his judgment upon themselves. Consider the Old Testament, full of blessings upon God's people and cursings upon others. God never changes. He always has and always will bless those who serve him and curse those who don't (Deuteronomy 28).

This blessing and cursing is not manifested in a different earthly life as karma. If you wonder why God's people sometimes seem to have hard lives, try a little exciting detective work for many different answers! Psalm 73, John 15:18-23, Hebrews 12:5-11, Job 23:10 and Ezekiel 18:30-32 all give part of the puzzle. Another piece is supplied by the apostle Paul who wrote:

> ...we never give up. Though our bodies are dying, our inner strength in the Lord is growing every day. These troubles and sufferings of ours are, after all, quite small and won't last very long. Yet, this short time of distress will result in God's richest blessing upon us forever and ever! So we don't look at what we can see right now, the troubles all around us, but we look forward to the joys in heaven which we have not yet seen. The troubles will soon be over, but the joys to come will last forever. (2 Corinthians 4:16-18) LB.

It does not work to try to prove the existence of karma by using the Bible verse "As you sow, so shall you reap." In this life, if you sow evil, evil will be done to you. Look around and see. A thief, for instance, will suffer for his thievery one way or another. If he dies without repenting and receiving Christ as his personal Savior, he will suffer eternally, reaping what he has sown. If anyone has Christ within, however, all is forgiven and what we have sown by faith are spiritual blessings which we shall reap eternally in heaven, in the presence of the Father. Heaven or hell are the only spiritual destinations in the Bible.

Christians are so blest! The "Great Transaction" lays all my sins on Christ; and his righteousness on me! What a trade! I can't live up to my own standards, let alone God's. Yet his Son within me makes me totally righteous. I know I have eternal life with God in the future — it depends on his goodness, not mine! Not what I **deserve,** but what I have sown by faith in Jesus Christ. I reap serenity and confidence in my future. I know whom I have believed. There is a former Hindu who says he used to have nightmares about being reincarnated as a bug or a plant or a handicapped child. Now that he is a Christian, he is reaping peace of mind which passes all understanding, a gift of the Prince of Peace.

Versus

Salvation by works — just take a look.
It's the oldest trick in Satan's book.
And what is reincarnation?
Same old theme, a variation!
Now see the love in Jesus' face,
Salvation not of works, but grace!

Here is yet another puzzle piece, this one from the Master himself:

> If the world hate you, ye know that it hated me before it hated you. If ye were of the world, the world would love its own; but because ye are not of the world, therefore, the world hateth you. Remember the word that I said unto you, the servant is not greater than his lord. If they have persecuted me, they will also persecute you; if they have kept my saying, they will keep yours also. But all these things will they do unto you for my name's sake, because they know not him that sent me. If I had not come and spoken unto them, they had not sin; but now they have no cloak for their sin. He that hateth me hateth my Father also (John 15:18-23).

> Let us hear the conclusion of the whole matter: Fear God [faith]; and keep his commandments [obedience]; for this is the whole duty of man. For God shall bring every work into judgment, with every secret thing, whether it be good, or whether it be evil (Ecclesiastes 12:13,14).

God **will** bring every work into judgment; on Judgment Day as he has said, not by karma as men may say.

SIX

Natural, Carnal, Spiritual

Most reincarnationists really want to believe that God is completely fair, and that he would not condemn people who did not know about him. What about that belief?

There are three kinds of people defined by the Bible:

(1) **Natural Man** — Born of the flesh, but not born of the Spirit, The center of this person's world is self. The natural man may seem appealing in many ways, but he has no real understanding of the Bible or of God. He is easy prey for deceptions which can reach him particularly through his intellect, emotions, will and body senses. This is illustrated in 1 Corinthians 2:13, 14:

> We speak not in the words which man's wisdom teacheth, but which the Holy Spirit teacheth, comparing spiritual things with spiritual. But the natural man receiveth not the things of the Spirit of God; for they are foolishness unto him, neither can he know them, because they are spiritually discerned.

(2) **Carnal Man** — A spiritually reborn person who follows after the flesh rather than hungering after things of the Lord. Though indwelt by the Holy Spirit, he has an extremely limited understanding because he refuses to give himself over to God, and may **never** grow spiritually. God's power is too great to be entrusted to such a one as this. So they remain spiritual "babes," able to digest only the simplest Bible truths, "milk," as described in the following:

> And I, brethren, could not speak unto you as unto spiritual, but as unto carnal, even as unto babes in Christ. I have fed you with milk, and not with solid food; for to this time ye were not able to bear it, neither yet are able. For ye are yet carnal; for whereas there is among you envying, and strife, and divisions, are ye not carnal, and walk as men? (1 Corinthians 3:1-3).

Christians who are given to carnality have done much irreparable damage to the image of God in the world. But they themselves will suffer the greater loss, as described in C.S. Lovett's brilliant work, *Why Die As You Are!*[1]

(3) **Spiritual Man** — Born again of the Spirit of God and filled with the Holy Spirit as described in Ephesians 5:18-20. This person's main desire is to glorify God. He wishes to put God first, last and always. To him the Bible is as necessary as food; and prayer is as vital as air to breathe. When he inevitably sins, he turns to Christ for forgiveness, accepts that forgiveness and goes on, aiming higher next time. His life is without frustration or fear, since he has placed all trust in God's perfect will and wisdom to direct every aspect of his life:

> For all who are led by the Spirit of God are sons of God (Romans 8:14 LB).
>
> The just shall live by faith (Galatians 3:11).

> And he has put his own Holy Spirit into our hearts as a proof to us that we are living with him and he with us...And as we live with Christ, our love grows more perfect and complete; so we will not be ashamed and embarrassed at the day of judgment, but can face him with confidence and joy, because he loves us and we love him too (1 John 4:13, 17 LB).

Romans 8:5-8 says this:

> Those who let themselves be controlled by their lower natures live only to please themselves, but those who follow after the Holy Spirit find themselves doing those things that please God. Following after the Holy Spirit leads to life and peace, but following after the old nature leads to death, because the old sinful nature within us is against God. It never did obey God's laws and it never will. That's why those who are still under the control of their old sinful selves, bent on following their old evil desires, can never please God (LB).

In spiritual matters, our "natural" instincts clearly bring us to disaster. Our thoughts and our ways seem natural and right to us, but it is God who is the authority:

> For my thoughts are not your thoughts, neither are your ways my ways, saith the Lord. For as the heavens are higher than the earth, so are my ways higher than your ways, and my thoughts than your thoughts (Isaiah 55:8,9).

Before Christ came, whoever believed he was coming was justified by their faith. Now that he has come, whoever believes that Christ came (and put their trust in him) are justified by their faith. But then, as now, it seems they must have heard of him before they could believe. Millions of people living at this moment have never heard of a Living God or his Son. It may seem natural and logical to us that they should be reincarnated so that they would have a chance to be saved. These uninformed people are not one bit more lost than the unbelieving American with a Bible in his house and a church down the street. They will have less explanation to give for their heathenism than he will. God defines a "heathen" as any unbeliever.

Are they who have never heard of God really lost? If they sincerely believe in the only religion they know, isn't this acceptable?

In his book *Are The Heathen Really Lost?,* Dick Hillis addresses this issue:

> Religion may be described as man's vain effort to quiet his conscience and satisfy his ego by attempting to reach Heaven. Salvation is God's great eternal program of reaching down and redeeming lost man. While men may have religion, they do not have salvation.... Christianity is more than a religion; it is a life. Religion consists of a set of rules and rituals. The founders of the religions are dead. The Giver of Salvation is alive....The world of today is a world of religion. Christ came to save men from sin and religion. Adam was the founder of the first religion. Upon being caught in sin in the garden, rather than cry to God for mercy, he sewed fig leaves together to cover his nakedness. He relied on his works rather than God's grace. From that day to this, man has been incurably religious. He continues to invent religions, thinking in this way to cover his spiritual nakedness. As the fig leaves of Adam's time did not cover sin, so all the religious acts of man today can not atone for sin. Religion can only leave a sinner hoping. Salvation makes a sinner sure....Of course, many people are sincerely religious, but they are sincerely wrong. We do not condemn them, but in the Gospel we show them a better way — the only way. God's way![2]

The Living Bible paraphrases Romans 2:9-14 this way:

> There will be sorrow and suffering for Jews and Gentiles alike who keep on sinning. But there will be glory and honor and peace from God for all who obey him, whether they are Jews or Gentiles. For God treats everyone the same. He will punish sin wherever it is found. He will punish the heathen when they sin, even though they never had God's written laws, for down in their hearts they know right from wrong. God's laws are written within them; their own conscience accuses them, or sometimes excuses them.

Jungle heathen and sidewalk heathen are exactly the same to God — lost sinners in need of a savior.

We may protest that the person who has never heard of the Savior can't possibly know about him. But God's word tells us they are without excuse for good reason:

> But God shows his anger from heaven against all sinful, evil men who push away the truth from them. For the truth about God is known to them instinctively; God has put this knowledge in their hearts. Since earliest times men have seen the earth and sky and all God made, and have known of his existence and great eternal power. So they will have no excuse [when they stand before God at Judgment Day]....Yes, they knew about him all right, but they wouldn't admit it or worship him or even thank him for all his daily care. And after a while they began to think up silly ideas of what God was like and what he wanted them to do. The result was that their foolish minds became dark and confused. Claiming themselves to be wise without God, they became utter fools instead (Romans 1:18-22 LB).

Jesus told the disciples, "Go ye, therefore, and teach all nations, baptizing them in the name of the Father, and of the

Son, and of the Holy Ghost (Matthew 28:19)." It has been estimated that fully one-half of all the people living on the earth at this moment have never heard the good news of Jesus Christ. If there were any other way to be reconciled to God, why would Jesus have told Christians to go to them? Millions of others have heard of Jesus, but have not accepted his sacrifice on their behalf. All of these people are truly lost and condemned since they are unable to meet God's requirement of perfection without the indwelling Son of God.

We admit that we are not perfect, but this admission is not limited to "civilized people."

Dr. J. B. Williams, for years a missionary in Africa, reveals that he has never met a person there who does not recognize their own guilt. Just as Romans 2:15 says, their own conscience tells them that they are guilty of wrong-doing. All admit that they do not live up even to their own standards.
"After all, salvation is not given to those who know what to do, unless they do it (Romans 2:15 LB)."

The fact is that the ancestors of these people **did** know the Living God, and turned away from him, preferring their sin.

Dr. Williams points to Romans 1:21, which says, **"when they knew God,** they glorified him not as God." He says the history of any nation can be followed back to a time when they knew God and deliberately turned away into darkness, teaching their children the false ways. The people of these nations are in darkness because their ancestors turned from the light.

Dr. Williams says that the ancient Levitical order and pattern is clearly shown, although corrupted, in the worship of primitive African tribes. He cites the way of applying blood to the doorposts of one tribe which is the same as the Passover way of the Jews. Another tribe uses a scapegoat once a year exactly as described in the Bible. All blood sacrifices of these tribes are based on customs handed down for generations, from the time when their ancestors **did** know the Living God. Some of these people even retained "ami," and use it to show religious agreement, exactly as we might say "amen." Romans 1:28 says, "So it was that when they gave God up and would not even acknowledge him, God gave them up to doing everything their evil minds could think of (LB)."

Each verse beginning with Romans 1:21 through verse 32 shows a further step downward away from God. These steps are exactly the ones followed by "heathen nations" whose descendants are pagans today.

But some who instinctively know that there is a "great someone" **do** seek God — and they do find him. Missionaries give abundant testimony of tribes or individuals who, after seeking the Creator, were reached with the Gospel under amazing circumstances.

One of my favorites among these true stories concerns a watchmaker in India. After completing a watch he held it up for final examination. As he looked, he considered how intricately that watch was made. It occurred to him that it could not just have happened. His eye strayed to the hand which held the watch, and he began to consider the wonders of the hand. He realized that nothing so marvelous could have just happened. With nothing else to go on, he began to worship the unseen "Hand-maker," and to ask him to reveal himself to the lowly watchmaker. As he persisted in his prayers, before long a missionary knocked at his door for directions. The "Hand-maker" was revealed and the watchmaker, who had never heard of God or his Son Jesus, was wonderfully saved!

Others have been wise enough to worship the "star-maker" instead of the stars, the "animal-maker" instead of the animal, etc. A college man I recently met told me that he had tried everything the world offered, and was still dissatisfied. Finally, in desperation and from his deepest heart he prayed, "God, if you are real, show me!" No sooner had he mentally uttered this prayer than a friend handed him a tract on finding God. No power or powers can ever convince that young man that God did not answer his prayer. Now he knows what satisfaction really is. And it keeps on getting better!

Helen Keller has revealed that even before anyone could communicate with her, she was aware of the presence of God. Although she was deaf, dumb and blind, she knew.

God is faithful and his promises so faithfully kept!

Jesus said, "Seek and ye shall find (Luke 11:9)." God promised, "And ye shall seek me, and find me, when you shall search for me with all your heart (Jeremiah 29:13)."

It has been said that in all the world, only one tribe has ever been found that was totally devoid of a worship concept. But this is not due to reincarnation; rather it testifies that God has written his laws on our hearts as he said he would. It takes a lot of hardening to become oblivious to sin. Our consciences work very well indeed. Our natural inclinations toward God are placed there by our maker. But all too often, in both individuals and whole civilizations, these inclinations have been perverted and directed away from God, rather than to him.

Satan uses our "natural" leanings toward religious ideas to his advantage more than we can imagine. The "natural man" in us urges us to "do good works" in an effort to get right with God. And Satan blinds the eyes of the natural man to keep us thinking that this approach to God can be effective. It seems "natural" and right to us that the person who leads an extremely moral life is **more** acceptable to God than the worst imaginable sinner. This false teaching has caused the downfall of more of mankind than any other. Martin Luther said that the most damnable and pernicious heresy that ever plagued the mind of man is that somehow he could deserve to live with an all-holy God. Since this is a hopeless approach to God, Satan has planted the idea in all false religions. This is why the jungle mother throws her baby to the crocodiles — in an effort to appease whatever gods she believes are there. This is why the church of the Dark Ages failed so miserably to show Christ's love in the world — even telling the people that they could actually buy the good deeds of others to tip the scales in their own favor. And this is why many moderns are desperately working for social reform or church busy-work — so pitifully often it's a vain effort to appease the god they have imagined to be the one true God. Our works do not save us:

> By grace are ye saved through faith; and that not of yourselves, it is the gift of God — Not of works, lest any man should boast (Ephesians 2:8,9).

But Satan wants us to think so because in that way we are helplessly lost.

The gift of God spoken of above can only be received by faith — which involves repentance. But before we can repent, we must recognize that we are guilty of something. If we do not acknowledge ourselves as sinful, we see no need to turn from sin.

"If we say that we have no sin, we deceive ourselves, and the truth is not in us (1 John 1:8)." The preferred meaning of the word repentance is literally to "turn from" the undesirable to the proper. If we repent, we actually turn from unbelief to belief. As John goes on to say in the verse following the one above:

> If we confess our sins, he is faithful and just to forgive us our sins, and to cleanse us from all unrighteousness (1 John 1:9).

The correction of sinful living follows, if the "turning from" unbelief is real. God does not force us to change; but, when we truly turn to belief, changing is what we **want** to do. This can take a long time. Repentance begins at conversion; the step by step "turning from" can take a lifetime.

The Bible says that there is rejoicing in heaven over every sinner who repents and turns to Christ in faith.

Repentance is not natural — we just naturally want our own way. "All we like sheep have gone astray; we have turned every one to his own way (Isaiah 53:6)." But only through repentance and the recognition that we need a Savior can we become spiritual rather than natural.

Reincarnation and karma seemed perfectly natural to me, but "natural" is precisely what's wrong with it! We must be spiritual, not natural, to dwell in God. "There is a way which seemeth right unto a man, but the end thereof are the ways of death. (Proverbs 14:12)."

A thousand reincarnations would be useless without a spiritual rebirth. Jesus said, "It is the spirit that giveth life; the flesh profiteth nothing (John 6:63)."

SEVEN

God's Love and/or Justice (Judgment Day, Resurrection)

As I said in the first chapter, one reason I accepted the idea of reincarnation was that I wanted with all my heart to believe in a God of **total** love and **total** fairness. But 100% of either one would exclude the other. If God were only love, it would be impossible for him to be fair. Many people have imagined in their own minds that God will take everyone to heaven, regardless of any standard or criteria. (What would heaven become then!) This imaginary concept of God would be completely unfair to those who believed his words that only his Son could provide salvation. It would also require that God be untrue to his own nature. It would cancel all the Bible's warnings of hell and eternal damnation; it would make the perfect God into a liar! If a judge does not abide by the law, he is an unfit judge. The Bible says, "Shall not the Judge of all the earth do right? (Genesis 18:25)"

On the other hand, none of us really wants a God who is only just, either. In this case, no one could ever dwell with God. We know deep in our hearts that we are not perfect — that we are sinful.

This dilemma is a real one, if we try to make God into the image we might want. Either way, we lose. Some people claim that karma is the solution, and that through karma, God has found a way to be both loving and fair. The Word of God does not say that karma is the way.

God IS both loving and fair. He is loving in that he provided a way for us to be forgiven. He is fair in that whoever accepts that way is forgiven and whoever rejects that way is doomed. Jesus claimed, "I am the way." No other will do.

In God's eyes, there are two classes of people. These are: (1) those who accepted God's Son (the saved, believers), and (2) those who have not (unbelievers). Both of these will be judged by God's standard and judgment for these two classes will be completely different.

The saved will be judged at the judgment seat of the one they have claimed as their master, the Lord Jesus Christ. He will judge what they have done for him, and what they have done for other reasons, such as self, pride, greed, etc. At this judgment we will learn the truth of the saying, "Only one life, twill soon be past, only what's done for Christ will last." This is what the Bible says:

> And no one can ever lay any other real foundation than the one we already have — Jesus Christ. But there are various kinds of other materials that can be used to build on that foundation. Some use gold and silver and jewels; and some build with sticks, and hay, or even straw! There is going to come a time of testing at Christ's Judgment Day to see what kind of material each builder has used. Everyone's work will be put through the fire so that all can see whether or not it keeps its value, and what was really accomplished. Then every workman who has built on the

foundation with the right materials, and whose work still stands, will get his pay. But if the house he has built burns up, he will have a great loss. He himself will be saved, but like a man escaping through a wall of flames (1 Corinthians 3:11-15 LB).

You are sending the material ahead every day, if you are a true Christian. The kind of material is strictly up to you. Jesus said:

But lay up for yourselves treasures in heaven, where neither moth nor rust doth corrupt, and where thieves do not break through nor steal; For where your treasure is, there will your heart be also (Matthew 6:20,21).

That is where you'll get the "gold and jewels and silver" —work done to glorify God instead of self, sent ahead and **laid up** by nobody else but you! These treasures will not be lost in the judgment fire, but, oh, those combustibles! They'll be gone and there'll be no reward for that kind of work.

As Thomas A' Kempis said, "Man considers the deeds, but God weighs the intentions."

Believers will have cause for tears as they see lost souls condemned whom they might have won; and as they see work done for selfish reasons go up in smoke. This is made plain in Revelation 21:4:

And God shall **wipe away all tears** from their eyes; and there shall be no more death, neither sorrow, nor crying, neither shall there be any more pain; for the former things are passed away.

For the unbelievers, there is an altogether different judgment. This is described in the Revelation of St. John, Chapter 20, verses 11 through 15:

And I saw a great white throne, and him that sat on it,

> from whose face the earth and the heaven fled away, and there was found no place for them. And I saw the dead, small and great, stand before God, and the books were opened; and another book was opened, which is the book of life. And the dead were judged out of those things which were written in the books, according to their works. And the sea gave up the dead that were in it, and death and hades delivered up the dead that were in them; and they were judged every man according to their works. And death and hades were cast into the lake of fire. This is the second death. And whosoever was not found written in the book of life was cast into the lake of fire.

How do we know that this judgment is only for those who have not put their trust in Christ?

First, Jesus said, "Whosoever believes in me has everlasting life." There will be no second death for them. But the people mentioned here are dead — they have no life in them. This judgment is for **all** who are the dead and **only** those who are dead, i.e., without the life of the Holy Spirit.

Second, in this judgment, the dead (unsaved) are judged according to their works since they have refused grace (the gift of God purchased by Christ). They have chosen to be judged by their works. Because works cannot possibly save them, all of these people are cast into the lake of fire. They have no building material laid up since they have refused the foundation, Jesus Christ. "For other foundation can no man lay than that which is laid, which is Jesus Christ (1 Corinthians 3:11)."

Third, in the above quote from Revelation, God tells us that death and hell were cast into the lake of fire and that this is the second death. (Those with **eternal** life cannot experience a second death.) The scriptures often mention first birth (physical) and second birth (spiritual). They tell us that we must die physical death once; now here is a second death which is not extermination, but continuing forever.

"It is appointed unto men once to die, but after this the judgment (Hebrews 9:27)." No room here for reincarnation. After the judgment comes the **second** death.

Some reincarnationists say that karma is our judgment; that is not what God says.

Reincarnation is also disproved by the biblical doctrine of the resurrection of the body.

The resurrection of the body seems to be an impossibility, but Jesus himself said that nothing is impossible for God.

Imagine a chemist busily working in his laboratory. He accidentally knocks a beautiful silver chalice into acid and it dissolves. But it's not a tragedy after all. He knows exactly how to reclaim every trace of the silver and when he has done so, he has it recast. It stands as lovely as ever. Since God is God, he knows exactly how to do everything that he has said he will do. He says we shall live once, die once, be raised up in our flesh, and judged; then rewarded or punished eternally. That's what God says. The resurrection of the body is coming because God says so:

> If the spirit of God, who raised up Jesus from the dead, lives in you, he will make your dying bodies live again after you die, by means of this same Holy Spirit living within you (Romans 8:11 LB).

In many places, the Bible teaches the resurrection of the body. Read Isaiah 26:19, Daniel 12:2, and David's words in Psalm 17:15.

Or consider the words of Job in Job 19:25-27:

> For I know that my redeemer liveth, and that he shall stand at the latter day upon the earth; And though after my skin worms destroy this body, yet in my flesh shall I see God, whom I shall see for myself, and mine eyes shall behold, and **not another;** though my heart be consumed within me.

Job's faith was unshakable. He knows that in his flesh he shall see God. If he had had many different bodies, which flesh would he wear to see God? Which eyes would he use? No, **not another;** his only flesh and his only eyes.

Job in his flesh truly shall see God and so shall you and I. Whoever we are, whatever our beliefs have been, we can know this — that ultimately **every** knee shall bow to the Lord, and every tongue shall confess to God. And every one of us shall give an account of himself to God (Romans 14:11 and 12).

The unbeliever who can truthfully say to God, "I never heard the name of Jesus" will have a far lighter degree of punishment than one who must confess, "I heard but did not accept." The Bible teaches that every one of us will recognize the justice of our judgment.

Revelation 14:10, 11 tells of the fate of those who worship the beast (Satan) rather than God:

> The same shall drink of the wine of the wrath of God, which is poured out without mixture into the cup of his indignation; and he shall be tormented with fire and brimstone in the presence of the holy angels, and in the presence of the Lamb; And the smoke of their torment ascendeth up forever and ever; and they have no rest day nor night.

Yes, it's hard to find a loving God in that picture. Hard, that is, until we think of the prevention which he prepared and the extensive warnings he has given. Hard until we think of this: to create all of the universe, the almighty God needed only to speak. But in order to save us from hell, he had to sink to becoming human, die an agonizing death, take our punishment himself, and rise from the dead physically. What a contrast! What love! And then to think that even though we reject his way, he still patiently and lovingly woos us by continually knocking at a door only we can open. "How shall we escape if we neglect so great a salvation? (Hebrews 2:3)."

When Jesus was asked a misleading question about the resurrection, he answered,

> Ye do err, not knowing the scriptures, nor the power of God... But as touching the resurrection of the dead, have ye not read that which was spoken unto you by God, saying, I am the God of Abraham, and the God of Issac, and the God of Jacob? God is not the God of the dead, but of the living (Matthew 22:29-32).

These three patriarchs, mentioned in the previous quote, believed in the coming Christ, so that they had life eternal. They "slept" but were not dead. Their souls existed still as the same men with the same names — the same men, and God said, "**I am** their God," not, "I **was** their God."

In John 11:25, Jesus says:

> I am the resurrection, and the life; he that believeth in me, though he were dead, yet shall he live. And whosoever liveth and believeth in me shall never die.

In John 3:36, Jesus says:

> He that believeth the Son hath everlasting life; and he that believeth not the Son shall not see life, but the wrath of God abideth on him.

In John 5:28-29, Jesus says:

> The hour is coming, in which all that are in the graves shall hear his voice, And shall come forth: they that have done good, unto the resurrection of life; and they that have done evil, unto the resurrection of damnation.

Do you long for a God who is both fair and loving? The Living Perfect God is both!

The prophet Zephaniah informs us of both sides of God's nature:

> And I will bring distress upon men, that they shall walk like blind men, because they have sinned against the Lord; and their blood shall be poured out like dust, and their flesh like the dung. Neither their silver nor their gold shall be able to deliver them in the day of the Lord's wrath, but the whole land shall be devoured by the fire of his jealousy; for he shall make a speedy riddance of all those who dwell in the land (Zephaniah 1:17-18).

Then in Chapter 3, Verse 17, the same prophet says:

> The Lord, thy God, in the midst of thee is mighty; he will save, he will rejoice over thee with joy; he will rest in his love, he will joy over thee with singing.

Jesus is the Savior, but does he save completely? Are all our sins really erased by his blood? Yes, if you believe in your heart and confess with your mouth, you shall be saved:

> Wherefore, he is able also to save them to the uttermost that come to God by him, seeing he ever liveth to make intercession for them (Hebrews 7:25).

If you have any doubts about the perfection of Christ's work on the cross, I suggest you read carefully and prayerfully Chapters 5 through 10 of the book of Hebrews. In this section of *Good News for Modern Man* (a translation which is approved by the Roman Catholic Church and also used by many Protestants), the following statements will be found:

> But Jesus lives on forever, and his work as priest does not pass on to someone else. And so he is able, now and always, to save those who come to God through him, because he lives for ever to plead with God for them. Jesus,

then, is the High Priest that meets our needs! (Hebrews 7:24-26 TEV).

He offered one sacrifice, once and for all, when he offered himself (Hebrews 7:27 TEV).

He took his own blood and obtained eternal salvation for us (Hebrews 9:12 TEV).

Through the eternal Spirit he offered himself as a perfect sacrifice to God. His blood will make our consciences clean from useless works, so that we may serve the living God (Hebrews 9:14 TEV).

But Christ did not go in to offer himself many times; for then he would have had to suffer many times ever since the creation of the world. Instead, he has appeared once and for all, when the ages of time are nearing the end, to remove sin through the sacrifice of himself. Everyone must die once, and after that be judged by God. In the same manner, Christ also was offered in sacrifice once to take away the sins of many. He will appear a second time, not to deal with sin, but to save those who are waiting for him (Hebrews 9:25-28).

With one sacrifice, then, he has made perfect forever those who are clean from sin. For the Holy Spirit also gives us his witness. First he says: 'This is the covenant that I will make with them. After those days, says the Lord: I will put my laws in their hearts, and I will write them on their minds.' And then he says, 'I will not remember their sins and wicked deeds any longer.' So when these have been forgiven, an offering to take away sins is no longer needed (Hebrews 10:14-18 TEV).

So God is both loving and just; and neither one excludes the other.

EIGHT

Second Chance? Death, Spiritual

High in the Rocky Mountains is a stream which is suddenly divided by a rock. Some water goes East and eventually to the Atlantic Ocean. Other water from the same stream goes West and ultimately into the Pacific Ocean. There is no indecision; the water must do one or the other. The separation point is that rock.

Jesus is the "Rock of Ages," separating God's children from the others. Failure to decide for him is a decision against him. The one who fails to decide will be swept, knowingly or not, to the lake of fire.

The basic conflict between reincarnation and Christianity is the question, "Is there another chance after death?"

Obviously, the reincarnationist's answer to that question is yes. Most would further this by adding, "as many as you need."

The Christian viewpoint can only be based on the Bible, since this is the source of God's information to us. While special revelations and prophecies are indeed being given to some

Christians today, what they are given by God never, never, never conflicts with the written word of God. If it does, the prophet is a false one. (See *True and False Prophets,*[1] by Don Basham.)

Jesus gave an outstanding teaching which addresses the question of whether we get a second chance to get right with God. He said in Luke 16:19-31,

> "There was a certain rich man, who was clothed in purple and fine linen, and fared sumptuously every day. And there was a certain beggar, named Lazarus, who was laid at his gate, full of sores, and desiring to be fed with the crumbs which fell from the rich man's table; moreover, the dogs came and licked his sores. And it came to pass that the beggar died, and was carried by the angels into Abraham's bosom; the rich man also died, and was buried; and in hell he lifted up his eyes, being in torments, and seeth Abraham afar off, and Lazarus in his bosom. And he cried and said, Father Abraham, have mercy on me, and send Lazarus, that he may dip the tip of his finger in water, and cool my tongue; for I am tormented in this flame. But Abraham said, Son, remember that thou in thy lifetime receivedst thy good things, and likewise Lazarus evil things; but now he is comforted, and thou art tormented. And beside all this, between us and you there is a great gulf fixed, so that they who would pass from here to you cannot; neither can they pass to us, that would come from there. Then he said, I pray thee, therefore, father, that thou wouldst send him to my father's house (for I have five brethren) that he may testify unto them, lest they also come into this place of torment. Abraham saith unto him, They have Moses and the prophets; let them hear them. And he said, Nay, father Abraham; but if one went unto them from the dead, they will repent. And he said unto

him, If they hear not Moses and the prophets, neither will they be persuaded, though one rose from the dead."

I had always assumed that this was a parable, but it is not. This is a true story told by Jesus as a warning. Other stories, if they are parables, say so. Check this out for yourself. No parable ever gives the name of a person involved. But Lazarus is named. Abraham, a real person, is quoted by Jesus. These three reasons are good evidence that this is no parable. I challenge you to read the passage carefully and find others.

Christ's account of the rich man and Lazarus teaches us a great deal. First, observe that neither had a second chance. Jesus says that Lazarus died; in the same breath, Jesus says he was carried to Abraham's bosom. No doubt this was paradise, where the souls of the redeemed waited for the work of Christ to be accomplished, so that they could enter heaven.

But the rich man died, and was buried. What a funeral he must have had! He had a big family (five brothers) and plenty of social status. But as soon as he landed in hell, he was tormented. He immediately lifted his eyes and saw a peaceful scene far away. His first words there were a cry for mercy. He, who had had no mercy on Lazarus while they were alive now wanted Lazarus to leave the peace he had found and come minister to him. We don't know whether Lazarus could hear his pleas, but Abraham could. This heartless man, so rich that he had feasted every day, now begged for just one drop of water. But Abraham reminded him of the life he will remember through all eternity — that he had had good things already, and, by implication, that he had not so much as shared his crumbs with a beggar. (In Luke 17:1 and 2, Jesus warns after finishing this account that offenses such as this must come to God's children like Lazarus, but those like the rich man will have woe, and it would have been better for them to have died rather than be one who offends God's own.) He will remember always with regret the materialism which he clung to rather than seek God's will.

Abraham was not being hard-hearted. He plainly says that there is a great gulf fixed between hades and paradise, so that no one could pass either way. The rich man did not beg to be reincarnated to warn his brothers or to just get out of there. Because it was not possible, he didn't even mention it. But he did become very missionary-minded. Since he knew very well he could not possibly get out, he begged that Lazarus be permitted to go back from the dead to warn his brothers not to come to that awful place where he was. But, in our terms, he was told, "They have the Bible, let them read that." The rich man knew his brothers well. He himself had had no time for scripture, and he knew that course to save them was very unlikely. But something very dramatic would — one from the dead! That request was also turned down. They would not listen even if one **did** return from the dead. If they won't hear the word of God, then they will not hear, no matter what. So the rich man's hopes were all empty —he had missed his only chance.

But, in fact, he had had hundreds of chances. He had known that Lazarus was by his gate every day. If he had humbled himself to speak to a beggar, even once, he might have heard about salvation. If he had truly studied the scriptures, he would have had a different eternity. His chances had been multiplied hundreds, and he had missed every last one. As he had hardened his heart to the beggar at the gate, so he had also hardened it to the persistent knocking of the Holy Spirit, as well as to the written word of God. He deserved hell, and hell is what he got.

"Shall not the Judge of all the earth do right? (Genesis 18:25)." Jesus is quoted by three gospel writers as saying, "I came not to call the righteous, but sinners to repentance (Matthew 9:13, Mark 2:17, Luke 5:32)." Yet there is **none** righteous (Romans 3:10); so the meaning here refers to the **self**-righteous, who will not see the need for their salvation. Jesus saves those who see their sins and repent, asking humbly for him to save them, since he is the only one qualified to save them.

Jesus, incidently, did rise from the dead, which the rich man thought would be proof of heaven and hell. Amazingly, Abraham's prophecy is correct. Many still refuse to be persuaded, even though one actually rose from the dead!

In the following selections, I have listed a few other statements Jesus made which disprove the theory of reincarnation for those who accept his words as authoritative. I have also indicated to whom he was speaking, where it makes a difference.

In Matthew 25:31-46, Jesus describes judgment day. He has separated the people, some like sheep on his right hand, some like goats on his left. To some people he says, in Verse 34, "Come, ye blessed of my Father, inherit the kingdom prepared for you from the foundation of the world." To others he says, in Verses 41-46,

> Depart from me, ye cursed, into everlasting fire....And these shall go away into everlasting punishment, but the righteous into life eternal.

Mark 16:16 says, "He that believeth and is baptized shall be saved; but he that believeth not shall be damned." (Notice he does say "damned," **not** "given another chance.")

John 5:28-29 says,

> The hour is coming, in which all that are in the graves shall hear his voice, and shall come forth: They that have done good [belief] unto the resurrection of life; and they that have done evil [unbelief] unto the resurrection of damnation.

In John 5:39-40 , Jesus says,

> Search the scriptures; for in them ye think ye have eternal life; and they are they which testify of me. And ye will not come to me, that ye might have life.

In John 11:23-37 (where Jesus and Martha are discussing her brother's death), Jesus says, "Thy brother shall rise again." Martha then says, "I know that he shall rise again in the resurrection at the last day." Jesus replies,

> I am the resurrection, and the life; he that believeth in me, though he were dead, yet shall he live. And whosoever liveth and believeth in me shall never die.

The raising of Lazarus was in part a picture of the resurrection of us all to come. Note that he was raised as himself, not a different body. The same with Tabitha in Acts 9:36-42, Jairus' daughter in Mark 5:22-43, and the son of the widow of Nain in Luke 7:11-17.

Certain claims have been made that the apostles of Jesus taught reincarnation. The following is a list of statements refuting those claims; with the name of the speaker or writer. Again, I have shown to whom the statement was made, if it makes any difference.

In Acts 24:15, Paul says, "...there shall be a resurrection of the dead, both of the just and unjust."

In 2 Corinthians 5:1 (LB), Paul says to the believers,

> For we know that when this tent we live in now is taken down — when we die and leave these bodies — we will have wonderful new bodies in heaven, homes that will be ours forevermore, made for us by God himself, and not by human hands.

In 2 Corinthians 5:6-10 (NEB), Paul says to the believers,

> Therefore we never cease to be confident. We know that so long as we are at home in the body we are exiles from the Lord; faith is our guide, we do not see him. We are confident, I repeat, and would rather leave our home in the body and go to live with the Lord. We therefore make it our ambition, wherever we are, here or there, to be

acceptable to him. For we must all have our lives laid open before the tribunal of Christ, where each must receive what is due to him for his conduct in the body, good or bad.

In 2 Thessalonians 1:7-10 (LB), Paul says to the believers,

> And so I would say to you who are suffering, God will give you rest along with us when the Lord Jesus appears suddenly from heaven in flaming fire with his mighty angels, bringing judgment on those who do not wish to know God, and who refuse to accept his plan to save them through our Lord Jesus Christ. They will be punished in everlasting hell, forever separated from the Lord, never to see the glory of his power, when he comes to receive praise and admiration because of all he has done for his people, his saints. And you will be among those praising him, because you have believed what we told you about him.

In 2 Peter 2:9, Peter says,

> The Lord knoweth how to deliver the godly out of temptations, and **reserve** the unjust unto the day of judgment to be punished.

In Revelation 20:10, John the Beloved says,

> And the devil that deceived them was cast into the lake of fire and brimstone, where the beast and the false prophet are, and shall be tormented day and night forever and ever.

Past tense is used in the above mentioned scripture passage because the event is so sure to happen. The judgment is prepared as the leader of the rebellion is disposed. Next, his followers are judged.

In Revelation 20:11-15 (LB), John the Beloved continues:

> And I saw a great white throne and the one who sat upon it, from whose face the earth and sky fled away, but

> they found no place to hide. I saw the dead, great and small, standing before God; and The Books were opened, including the Book of Life. And the dead were judged according to the things written in The Books, each according to the deeds he had done. The oceans surrendered the bodies buried in them; and the earth and the underworld gave up the dead in them. Each was judged according to his deeds. And Death and Hell were thrown into the Lake of Fire. This is the Second Death — the Lake of Fire. And if anyone's name was not found recorded in the Book of Life, he was thrown into the Lake of Fire.

In this section, note that the throne denotes authority and power. Its whiteness tells us that it is flawless and perfect. The judge who sits in this court is so majestic and powerful that even the very earth and sky flee from his presence, as if there was a place to hide! The dead, both great and small, must stand before this judge. (If reincarnation were true, there could be no distinguishing between great and small.) Each person was judged according to their deeds. (**This** is where their deeds are judged, **not** by "karma.") The oceans surrendered the bodies buried in them. (Each dead body waits for this judgment, regardless of where it has been.) Each body is a different person, and each one is judged, according to his works. The lake of fire is the second (not the hundredth or any other number) death. Each person has **one** name — if it is not in the book of life, he or she is cast into the lake of fire.

The above listings disprove all claims that the New Testament teaches reincarnation. The following ones do the same based on the Old Testament. Once again, I have mentioned the name of speaker and addressee if important to the context.

In Exodus 34:6-7, God says to Moses,

> The Lord, the Lord God, merciful and gracious, long-suffering, and abundant in goodness and truth, keeping

> mercy for thousands, forgiving iniquity and transgression and sin, and who will by **no means** clear the guilty.

The guilty, referred to above, are those who refuse forgiveness. The innocent are those who accept God's forgiveness through Christ. The words "no means," mentioned above, mean that there is only one way the guilty can become innocent, and it is not through karma, nor reincarnation, nor purgatory, nor "good works".

Job 10:19-21 says,

> I should have been as though I had not been; I should have been carried from the womb to the grave. Are not my days few? Cease then, and let me alone, that I may take comfort a little, before I go to the place from which I shall not return, even to the land of darkness and the shadow of death.

Job 14:10-12 says,

> But man dieth, and wasteth away; yea, man giveth up the ghost and where is he? As the waters fail from the sea, and the flood decayeth and drieth up; So man lieth down, and riseth not. Till the heavens be no more, they shall not awake, nor be raised out of their sleep.

(But heaven and earth shall pass away, then come the resurrections and judgments.)

Job 14:14 says, "If a man die, shall he live again? All the days of my appointed time will I wait, till my change come." (Our bodies must all wait until the appointed time for the resurrection.)

Job 19:26 says, "In my flesh shall I see God."

In Psalm 39:13, David says to the Lord, "Oh, spare me, that I may recover strength, before I depart and am no more."

In Psalm 49:17-19 (LB), David speaks of those who trust in wealth rather than trust God:

> For when they die they carry nothing with them! Their honors will not follow them. Though a man calls himself happy all through his life — and the world loudly applauds success — yet in the end he dies like everyone else, and enters eternal darkness.

Solomon speaks in the following passages,

> For the living know that they shall die; but the dead know not anything, neither have they any more a reward; for the memory of them is forgotten. Also their love, and their hatred, and their envy are now perished; neither have they any more a portion forever in any thing that is done under the sun (Ecclesiastes 9:5,6).

> Whatsoever thy hand findeth to do, do it with thy might; for there is no work nor device, nor knowledge, nor wisdom in the grave, whither thou goest (Ecclesiastes 9:10).

> Rejoice, O young man, in thy youth, and let thy heart cheer thee in the days of thy youth, and walk in the ways of thine heart, and in the sight of thine eyes; but know thou, that for all these things God will bring thee into judgment (Ecclesiastes 11:9).

In Ecclesiastes 12:13-14, Solomon upholds faith plus works and foretells the sure judgment day:

> Let us hear the conclusion of the whole matter: Fear God [faith], and keep his commandments [works]; for this is the whole duty of man. For God shall bring every work into judgment, with every secret thing, whether it be good, or whether it be evil.

Isaiah 64:6 says,

> But we are all as an unclean thing, and all our righteousnesses are as filthy rags; and we all do fade as a leaf, and our iniquities, like the wind, have taken us away.

In Ezekiel 18:4, the Lord God says to Ezekiel, "Behold, all souls are mine; the soul that sinneth, it shall die."

In Ezekiel 18:31-32, the Lord God says to the people through Ezekiel,

> Cast away from you all your transgressions, by which ye have transgressed, and make yourselves a new heart and a new spirit; for why will ye die?... For I have no pleasure in the death of him that dieth, saith the Lord God; wherefore, turn yourselves, and live.

Daniel 12:2 says,

> "And many of those who sleep in the dust of the earth shall awake, some to everlasting life, and some to shame and everlasting contempt."

The Bible is the Christian statement of faith. Opposing ideas cannot be considered Christian. Is it possible, then, to hold to both beliefs — reincarnation and Christianity? No, because they conflict; any attempt to combine them is illogical. They are totally incompatible. Jesus said,

> "No man can serve two masters; for either he will hate the one, and love the other; or else he will hold to the one, and despise the other (Matthew 6:24)."

"Choose this day whom we will serve... but as for me and my house, we will serve the Lord (Joshua 24:15)."

NINE

Death, Physical

Surely any discussion on reincarnation would be pointless without considering our attitudes toward death.

An unspoken curiosity, at least, about death is implied if there is an interest in reincarnation. Judging by television and movies, it seems that we are preoccupied with death. On the other hand, death is rarely mentioned in conversation. On a personal level, it is still a fairly taboo subject to be treated most gingerly. Elderly people in a nursing home for incurables were asked on a questionnaire what they would most like to talk about. Their answer was death. Everybody avoids it, including their doctors. But these folks say that the fear of the unknown is worse by far and find no comfort in avoiding the topic.

The Bible is a vast storehouse of information about death. Let's see in part what the Bible says about physical death.

"It is appointed unto men once to die, but after this the judgment (Hebrews 9:27)." This is a flat and simple statement which surely needs no embellishment. This judgment is graphically discussed in Chapter Seven.

The *New Scofield Reference Bible* has this note at Hebrews 9:27:

> Death (physical), Summary: (1) Physical death is a consequence of sin (Gen. 3:19), and the universality of death proves the universality of sin (Rom. 5:12-14). (2) Physical death affects the body only, and is not cessation of existence or of consciousness (Hab. 2:5, note; Lk. 16:23, note; Rev. 6:9-10). (3) All physical death ends in the resurrection of the body. (See Resurrection, Job 19:25; 1 Cor. 15:52, note). (4) Because physical death is a consequence of sin, it is not inevitable to the redeemed (Gen. 5:24; 1 Cor. 15:51-52; 1 Th. 4:15-17). (5) Physical death has for the Christian a peculiar qualification. It is called "sleep," because his body may be awakened at any moment (Phil. 3:20-21; 1 Th. 4:14-18). (6) The soul and spirit live, independently of the death of the body, which is described as a "tabernacle" (tent), in which the "I" dwells, and which may be put off (2 Cor. 5:1-8; cp. 1 Cor. 15:42-44; 2 Pet. 1:13-15). And (7) at the Christian's death he is at once "with the Lord" and his body awaits resurrection at the return of Christ (2 Cor. 5:1-8; Phil. 1:23; 1 Th. 4:13-17).[1]

Most people are genuinely puzzled by the attitude of Christians who calmly face their own death. Even more confusing is their quiet acceptance of the death of a loved one. A cousin sent me a moving poem written by a young mother after the accidental death of her little boy. It sang with hope. The day after the accident, the parents were in Sunday service as usual, praising the Lord through their grief. Yes, they truly loved their son. They were neither stupid nor in shock. They were simply standing on the promises of God. They knew their son to be now in a better place, namely heaven. Note that word, "knew." It was not a matter of hoping or guessing — it was a matter of knowledge. How could they possibly know this?

> These things have I written unto you that believe on the name of the Son of God, that ye may **know** that ye have eternal life (1 John 5:13).

Reincarnation assumes that everyone has eternal life, and the soul, if it does well, will eventually in some way be with God. But there's the hitch. Doing well. Just how good is good enough to dwell with God? A central fact of eternal life as taught by the Bible is that it is a totally free gift. "The wages of sin is death, but the gift of God is eternal life (Romans 6:23)." The parents I just mentioned were not convinced that their son was perfect, and so eligible for heaven. Just the opposite is true. They knew that he was not perfect, for none of us is. "All have sinned and come short of the glory of God (Romans 3:23)." To dwell with God, perfection is required. As light and darkness cannot inhabit the same place at the same time, neither can God's holiness and man's sinfulness coexist. The boy's entry into heaven did not hinge on **his** goodness, but on Christ's.

> For by grace are ye saved, through faith, and that not of yourselves, it is the gift of God, not of works, lest any man should boast (Ephesians 2:8-9).

The boy had placed his trust solely on Jesus Christ and had been reborn. The parents know this and no comfort could have been greater to their hearts. They know that he had made a decision to accept the gift. They know without a shadow of a doubt that Christ's goodness is sufficient; that since the Holy Spirit indwelt their boy, he is accounted as perfect in God's sight. They have no fear for him, because they have confidence in the One in whom they have put their trust. They have perfect peace of mind. They know they'll be together in heaven someday. They have no fear of being wrong since they believe God, not man.

King David had this same confidence centuries ago when his infant son died. He said, "Can I bring him back again? I shall go to him, but he shall not return to me (2 Samuel 12:23)." Like these modern parents, David had no fear for the child. "Perfect love casteth out fear (1 John 4:18)."

Surely fear is the opposite of peace. Jesus comforted his disciples with these words:

> I am leaving you with a gift — peace of mind and heart! And the peace I give isn't fragile like the peace the world gives. So don't be troubled or afraid (John 14:27 LB).

Do we want to cling to this world for fear of the next?

> Do not be worried and upset, Jesus told them. Believe in God, and believe also in me. There are many rooms in my Father's house, and I am going to prepare a place for you. I would not tell you this if it were not so. And after I go and prepare a place for you, I will come back and take you to myself, so that you will be where I am (John 14:1-3 TEV).

Promises like this from anyone else would be impossible to believe. But close examination of the life, words, deeds, miracles, death and resurrection of Jesus reveal him as one to be trusted. Some people say that he was not the Christ, but he was a good man. How could he be good if he spoke lies? He said, "I am the way, I am the truth, I am the life; no one goes to the Father except by me (John 14:6 TEV)." If it is not true, it is a monstrous lie, and no good man could have uttered it! No, Jesus was more than merely a good man. Just as the Bible teaches, Jesus is both human and divine (Luke 24:39).

By his perfect life, which no mere man could live, Jesus showed himself to be God. By his power over nature and disease and demonic forces, Jesus showed himself to be God. By his promises and claims about himself, Jesus showed himself to be God. By his statement that the scriptures were about him, Jesus claimed to be God (John 5:39). By his assertions of his relationship to the Father, Jesus showed himself to be God. After his resurrection, when doubting Thomas finally believed, he worshipped Jesus, calling him "My Lord and my God (John 20:28)." Jesus accepted this and did not rebuke it, showing that he is God. By his promise that he will indwell each believer, thus granting them eternal life, Jesus claimed to be God (John 6:47).

Why is Christianity different from other religions? This is a question we hear over and over again. But it is as inappropriate a question as asking a baby, "How's your wife?" True Christianity is not a religion at all — it is a Person —the indwelling Person of Jesus Christ. The living of the Christian life is a result of this indwelling, not a substitute for it.

The point is that if we put our trust in Jesus Christ, we need have no fear of death at all. He offers a sure and positive hope of the life to come. Hope placed in reincarnation is shaky and based on the words of people with pitifully small credentials compared to those of Jesus. Paul looked forward joyfully to living with his Master. "For to me to live is Christ, and to die is gain (Philippians 1:21)." He was willing to live his life for Jesus; he was willing also to die a death for Jesus.

In 1 Corinthians 15, Paul defined for us much of what we need to know about death.

> Now let me remind you, brothers, of what the Gospel really is, for it has not changed — it is the same Good News I preached to you before. You welcomed it then and still do now, for your faith is squarely built upon this wonderful message; and it is this Good News that saves you if you still firmly believe it, unless, of course, you never really believed it in the first place.
>
> I passed on to you right from the first what had been told to me, that Christ died for our sins just as the Scriptures said he would, and that he was buried, and that

three days afterwards he arose from the grave, just as the prophets foretold. He was seen by Peter and later by the rest of 'the Twelve.' After that he was seen by more than five hundred Christian brothers at one time, most of whom are still alive, though some have died by now. Then James saw him and later all the apostles. Last of all I saw him too, long after the others....

But tell me this! Since you believe what we preach, that Christ rose from the dead, why are some of you saying that dead people will never come back to life again? For if there is no resurrection of the dead, then Christ must still be dead. And if he is still dead, then all our preaching is useless and your trust in God is empty, worthless, hopeless; and we apostles are all liars because we have said that God raised Christ from the grave, and of course that isn't true if the dead do not come back to life again. If they don't, then Christ is still dead, and you are very foolish to keep on trusting God to save you, and you are still under condemnation for your sins; in that case, all Christians who have died are lost! And if being a Christian is of value to us only now in this life, we are the most miserable of creatures.

But the fact is that Christ did actually rise from the dead, and has become the first of millions who will come back to life again some day.

Death came into the world because of what one man (Adam) did, and it is because of what this other man (Christ) has done that now there is the resurrection from the dead. Everyone dies because all of us are related to Adam, being members of his sinful race, and wherever there is sin, death results. But all who are related to Christ will rise again. Each, however, in his own turn: Christ rose first; then when Christ comes back, all his people will become alive again....

But someone may ask, 'How will the dead be brought back to life again? What kind of bodies will they have?' What a foolish question! You will find the answer in your own garden! When you put a seed into the ground it doesn't grow into a plant unless it 'dies' first. And when the green shoot comes up out of the seed, it is very different from the seed you first planted. For all that you put into the ground is a dry little seed of wheat, or whatever it is you are planting, then God gives it a beautiful new body—just the kind he wants it to have; a different kind of a plant grows from each kind of seed. And just as there are different kinds of seeds and plants, so also there are different kinds of flesh. Humans, animals, fish, and birds are all different.

The angels in heaven have bodies far different from ours, and the beauty and the glory of their bodies is different from the beauty and glory of ours. The sun has one kind of glory while the moon and stars have another kind. And the stars differ from each other in their beauty and brightness.

In the same way, our earthly bodies which die and decay are different from the bodies we shall have when we come back to life again, for they will never die. The bodies we have now embarrass us for they become sick and die; but they will be full of glory when we come back to life again. Yes, they are weak, dying bodies now, but when we live again they will be full of strength. They are just human bodies at death, but when they come back to life they will be superhuman bodies. For just as there are natural, human bodies, there are also supernatural spiritual bodies.

The Scriptures tell us that the first man, Adam, was given a natural, human body but Christ is more than that, for he was life-giving Spirit.

First, then, we have these human bodies and later on God gives us spiritual, heavenly bodies. Adam was made from the dust of the earth, but Christ came from heaven above. Every human being has a body just like Adam's, made of dust, but all who become Christ's will have the same kind of body as his — a body from heaven. Just as each of us now has a body like Adam's, so we shall some day have a body like Christ's.

I tell you this, my brothers: an earthly body made of flesh and blood cannot get into God's kingdom. These perishable bodies of ours are not the right kind to live forever. But I am telling you this strange and wonderful secret: we shall not all die, but we shall all be given new bodies! It will all happen in a moment, in the twinkling of an eye, when the last trumpet is blown. For there will be a trumpet blast from the sky and all the Christians who have died will suddenly become alive, with new bodies that will never, never die; and then we who are still alive shall suddenly have new bodies too. For our earthly bodies, the ones we have now that can die, must be transformed into heavenly bodies that cannot perish but will live forever.

When this happens, then at last this Scripture will come true — 'Death is swallowed up in victory.' O death, where then your victory? Where then your sting? For sin — the sting that causes death — will all be gone; and the law, which reveals our sins, will no longer be our judge. How we thank God for all of this! It is he who makes us victorious through Jesus Christ our Lord!

So, my dear brothers, since future victory is sure, be strong and steady, always abounding in the Lord's work, for you know that nothing you do for the Lord is ever wasted as it would be if there were no resurrection (1 Corinthians 15 LB).

Jesus said,

> I say emphatically that anyone who listens to my message and believes in God who sent me has eternal life, and will never be damned for his sins, but has already passed out of death into life. And I solemnly declare that the time is coming, in fact, it is here, when the dead shall hear my voice — the voice of the Son of God — and those who listen shall live (John 5:24-25 LB).

So Jesus Christ says that those who believe in him have eternal life already in their possession.

A question — how long will eternal life last? It seems to be a silly question, but still some will try to claim that eternal life is only temporary. They can say what they like. Eternal means eternal.

The last verse of the wonderful old hymn, "Amazing Grace," beautifully describes it:

When we've been there ten thousand years,
Bright shining as the sun,
We've no less days to sing God's praise
Than when we'd first begun.[2]

In no way will this eternity be boring! The Lord has said that his people will reign with him (Revelation 5:10). St. Paul quotes the prophet Isaiah when he joyfully assures us,

> Eye hath not seen, nor ear heard, neither have entered into the heart of man, the things which God hath prepared for them that love him (1 Corinthians 2:9, Isaiah 64:4).

The self-preservation instinct of a Christian is as strong as anyone else's. The Christian is aware that the longer he lives, the more service he can be to the Lord. But, when death comes, victory and home-coming have arrived. It's then time to meet face-to-face the One who loves you more than words can tell. Surely death under these circumstances is nothing to fear!

Those who have had "second birth" will never have the "second death."

A complete study on death as discussed in the scriptures is not possible here. By the use of a good Bible concordance, you could easily plan your own study on death or any other topic.

Just sincerely ask God each time you begin to show you what he wants you to learn. If you mean it, he will answer.

TEN

Origen and Justinian

I think what finally cemented my belief in reincarnation more than anything else was the fascinating story of Origen and Emperor Justinian.

I had never heard of Origen; few people have. Yet Origen was such a prolific writer (some 6,000 books) that St. Jerome asks, "Which of us can read all that he has written?"

Origen (A.D. 185-254), according to my research,[1] was an early church leader greatly influenced by the teachings of Plato, a reincarnationist. Origen appears to have taught reincarnation, successive world orders, the transformation of angels into human souls, and that Jesus of Nazareth was special only because the Christ had sanctified his body by inhabiting it!

The point is that Origen's writings were many and his influence great, yet almost none of his works still exist. The teachings listed above are all anti-Biblical, to put it mildly. Why have they not survived?

Apparently for two hundred years, Origen's teachings did survive; then came Justinian. Justinian (483-565), as Emperor of the Roman Empire had great power. Much has been said about his wife, Theodora, and her evil influence over her equally evil husband. Whatever their reasons were, they caused Origen's works to be banned and destroyed. Justinian, we are told, kidnapped Pope Virgillius, set up the Fifth Ecumenical Council, loaded it with bishops who would vote the "proper" way, excluded all others (even the Pope), and rammed through the decrees which declared Origen's teachings anathema.

Would the Christian church today be teaching from Origen's writings if Justinian had not done these things? Would some of his writings even have found their way into the Bible itself? Many reincarnationists believe that Justinian caused the Bible to be changed. They say that all copies of scripture were known, accounted for, and changed to agree with Justinian's wishes. They cite the great power of the Emperor, and think that the Bible was carefully gone over to eliminate "most" references to reincarnation.

However, these ideas, when thought through more carefully, prove to be untrue.

First, consider the logistics of rounding up each copy of scripture for changing. Every monastery had a manuscript room. By the time of Justinian, hundreds of monks, in hundreds of places, for hundreds of years, had painstakingly copied from earlier manuscripts. Could they really all be tracked down and altered? Would all these people blithely turn over the previous work which they considered God's word? While some might have given in to an evil monarch, what a fight most would have put up! Think how they would have protected and hidden the cherished manuscripts!

Second, there is the historical fact of the Jews. For more than two thousand years, by the time of Justinian, the Jews had been carefully and reverently preserving their scriptures. They would not have changed them voluntarily. Neither could they have been forced by Justinian to change them, since his power was limited. The Western Roman Empire was a shambles when he became Emperor. The Jews were dispersed all over the known world, with untold thousands beyond Roman reach.

There is even evidence that Justinian may have been a Christian intent on eliminating heresies in his empire. This is the view taken by World Book Encyclopedia.[2] If this view is correct, it is doubly sure that he would not have changed the word of God.

Third, we have not reckoned with the power of God. It is ludicrous to imagine that an Almighty God would be powerless to preserve his message to the world. We have the word of Jesus Christ himself who tells us, "Heaven and earth shall pass away, but my words shall not pass away (Matthew 24:35)." Peter also spoke of this permanence: "...the word of God which liveth and abideth forever... the word of the Lord endureth forever (1 Peter 1:23-25)." Indeed, the everlasting nature of the words of God are taught throughout the Bible. Jesus said with finality, "The scripture cannot be broken (John 10:35)." The Dead Sea Scrolls are proving that no changes have been made.[3]

Surely, God, the all-powerful, used Justinian in this case to accomplish his purposes. This is a principle illustrated repeatedly in the Bible. For instance, in Exodus 7:3, Pharaoh's heart was hardened to show the sovereign power of God to Israel, to Egypt and to us.

For various reasons, God has allowed various kinds of people to rule. Daniel the prophet proclaimed of God, "He changeth the times and the seasons; he removeth kings, and setteth up kings (Daniel 2:21)." The story of Nebuchadnezzar in Daniel 4:28-37 is an interesting case in point.

At his trial, Jesus bluntly told Pilate, "Thou couldest have no power at all against me, except it were given thee from above (John 19:11)."

Justinian had power because he had been allowed power by God. If it were not for Justinian's interference, Origen's writings may have been added to God's word — although his writings were not inspired by the Holy Spirit. They would have contradicted the Bible on the doctrines of forgiveness, eternal life, the purpose of life, the identity of Christ, and salvation itself.

Perhaps we fail to understand God's method of using a tyrant to accomplish his purpose, but his ways are not our ways, his thoughts are not our thoughts (Isaiah 55:8). If we could understand him, he would be more our equal than our God. What would be the good of a God no wiser or greater than we?

ELEVEN

Elijah and John the Baptist: Jacob and Esau

Perhaps the most common Bible reference used in an effort to prove reincarnation is the correlation between Elijah and John the Baptist.

The last book of the Old Testament was written by Malachi in the fifth century before Christ. Malachi 4:5 **seems** to prophesy the ministry of John the Baptist. Here the word of God says, "Behold, I will send you Elijah, the prophet, before the great and terrible day of the Lord."

With this as background, let's move forward to Matthew 17:

> Jesus taketh Peter, James, and John, his brother, and bringeth them up to an high mountain privately, and was transfigured before them; and his face did shine like the sun, and his raiment was as white as light. And behold, there appeared unto them Moses and Elijah talking with him. Then answered Peter, and said unto Jesus, Lord, it is good for us to be here; if thou wilt, let us make here three

> booths; one for thee, and one for Moses, and one for Elijah. While he yet spoke, behold, a bright cloud overshadowed them; and behold, a voice out of the cloud, which said, This is my beloved Son, in whom I am well pleased; hear ye him. And when the disciples heard it, they fell on their face, and were very much afraid.

After all this, they **knew** without question that Jesus was the promised Messiah. But they wondered on the way down the mountain about Malachi's prophecy. Since this is the Lord, where is Elijah?

Jesus dealt first with what they had already learned; that he was the Messiah, and as such, much greater than mere prophets. He did not want it widely known yet who he was (not until he was raised again from the dead), and sternly told them not to tell anyone about the vision they had seen.

Apparently they did not pursue the matter any further, but they still wanted to know about Elijah.

> The disciples said to Jesus, 'Why then say the scribes that Elijah must first come?' Jesus answered ... 'Elijah truly shall first come, and restore all things. But I say unto you that Elijah is come already, and they knew him not, but have done to him whatsoever they desired. Likewise shall also the Son of Man suffer of them.' Then the disciples understood that he spoke unto them of John the Baptist (Matthew 17:10-13).

Perhaps the Lord felt that they had had enough for one day. He did not choose at this time to make clear to them that he would truly have to die and would eventually return a second time. On another such occasion, Jesus said to them, "I have many things yet to say unto you, but ye cannot bear them now (John 16:12)."

Since the disciples did not understand the fact of two

comings, they did not understand the fact of two forerunners. Malachi's prophecy told of Elijah instead of John the Baptist who was **like** Elijah.

This does not contradict what Jesus said, since he used both future and past tenses in his answer. Careful reading shows that **Elijah shall** come.

As I said earlier, before my rebirth I had felt free to pick and choose which Bible verses to believe or reject. Like most reincarnationists, I jumped to the conclusion, based on this conversation, that even Jesus believed in reincarnation. But, if I had been willing to study, I would have found Luke 1:17 and John 1:21 (not to mention the whole context of Jesus' teachings).

In Luke 1, the angel Gabriel explained to Zacharias, the father of John the Baptist, that he was to have a son and what that child would do:

> And he shall go before him (the Lord) in the spirit and power of Elijah — to make ready a people prepared for the Lord. (Luke 1:17)

Notice that Gabriel did not say that this **was** Elijah, but that he would have the **spirit** and **power** of Elijah. Bear in mind that soul and spirit are entirely different.

Later, during his ministry, John the Baptist was asked point-blank whether he was Elijah (John 1:21). His answer? "I am not." Could it be clearer than that? Then he told them clearly who he was, as prophesied in Isaiah 40:3 when he said, "Make straight the way of the Lord." Notice he did not mention the Malachi prophecy. He knew which forerunner he was: the one prophesied by Isaiah.

Isaiah 40:3 says,

> The voice of him that crieth in the wilderness, Prepare ye the way of the Lord, make straight in the desert a highway for our God.

This was to be the mission of John the Baptist. It was Isaiah's prophecy, not Malachi's, that he was to fill. How do we know? See Matthew 3:3:

> In those days came John the Baptist, preaching in the wilderness of Judea, and saying, Repent; for the kingdom of heaven is at hand. For this is he that was spoken of by the prophet, Isaiah, saying, The voice of one crying in the wilderness, Prepare ye the way of the Lord, make his paths straight. (Matthew 3:1-3)

The *New Scofield Reference Bible* has an enlightening note for Matthew 17:10. It says:

> Compare Malachi 3:1, 4:5-6; Matthew 11:14; Mark 9:11-13; Luke 1:17. All the passages must be taken together. (1) Christ confirms the specific and still unfulfilled prophecy of Malachi 4:5-6: 'Elijah truly shall first come and restore all things.' Here, as in Malachi, the prediction fulfilled in John the Baptist, and that yet to be fulfilled in Elijah, are kept distinct. (2) But John the Baptist had come already, and with a ministry so completely in the spirit and power of Elijah's future ministry (Luke 1:17) that in a typical sense, it could be said: 'Elijah is come already.' Compare Matthew 10:40; Philemon 12, 17, where the same thought of identification, although still preserving personal distinction, occurs (compare John 1:21).[1]

In other words, John was not the same man as Elijah. Elijah **is still** to come, before the "great and terrible day of the Lord," exactly as Malachi 4:5 says. John the Baptist, who was born just before Jesus, was the messenger "crying in the wilderness, make straight the way of the Lord, as said the prophet **Isaiah."** These are the words of John the Baptist himself when he was asked who he was (John 1:23). John the Baptist came in the **spirit** of Elijah, the same **kind** of man; so much so that Jesus could say he "came already." It was to identify John the Baptist as his forerunner that Jesus said, "Elijah is come already."

Since Moses, Jews at the time of Christ had been celebrating the Passover every year. For generations, they had included (and still do) a touching way to show that they await Elijah, whose appearance would precede the Messiah's coming. At each home when Passover is celebrated, an extra place is set at the table. No one may use it, as it is reserved for Elijah. During the celebration, a child of the family goes to the door to see if Elijah has arrived. What child would not keenly feel the disappointment to realize that Elijah is not there, and that the people must wait another year to look for him? The hope for Elijah's coming is kept very much alive. Small wonder, then, that the disciples questioned Jesus; now that they knew that he was the Messiah, why had they not seen Elijah before they saw Christ?

Clearly, the Jews were uncertain as to how Elijah would appear, since every home expected him, full grown, to come for their Passover supper. So when Jesus eulogized John the Baptist, he told them, "And **if** ye will receive it, this is Elijah, who was to come. He that hath ears to hear, let him hear (Matthew 11:14-15)." **If** only they would receive it, Jesus was identifying John the Baptist as his first forerunner.

God knew that the Jews were looking for a victorious king to save them from Roman rule. He knew that they would reject a humble suffering Savior who must set up a spiritual kingdom to save souls. If Elijah had come prematurely, the earthly kingdom would have had to begin, and souls would not have been saved by the sacrifice of Christ. So John the Baptist was sent in the **spirit** of Elijah; the same kind of man.

John the Baptist, the first forerunner, actually had appeared before Jesus. Not only did his ministry begin first, he was also born first. His mother Elisabeth was well along in her pregnancy before Mary came to tell of hers (Luke 1:39-56).

John the Baptist was a man born (Luke 1), but Elijah who had been born long before, had **not** died. The scriptures tell us that he was taken to heaven on a "fiery chariot" (2 Kings 2:11). (There were fifty-one witnesses to this event!) Could a man still living be reincarnated?

Just before Elijah was taken to heaven, Elisha and he had a very interesting conversation. Elisha asked Elijah, "I pray thee, let a double portion of thy spirit be upon me (2 Kings 2:9)." Elijah answered,

> Thou hast asked a hard thing. Nevertheless, if thou see me when I am taken from thee, it shall be unto thee; but if not, it shall not be so.

After he watched Elijah's departure, Elisha succeeded him as prophet. His request was granted, for the sons of the prophets who were watching said, "The spirit of Elijah doth rest on Elisha (2 Kings 2:15)."

This clearly meant his power, his mission; not his soul. Elisha became the same **kind** of man as Elijah, just as John the Baptist did, many years later.

We must bear in mind that Christ is to have a forerunner in **both** of his physical visits to earth. The first was John the Baptist, **next will be Elijah,** just as Malachi 4:5 says.

Let's look again at Malachi 4:5. It says, "Behold, I will send you Elijah, the prophet, before the coming of the great and terrible day of the Lord." I also submit that John the Baptist could not be the same man as Elijah, since the great and terrible day of the Lord has not yet arrived. That day is described in many places in the Bible, as in Joel 3:9-16. The Battle of

Armageddon will mean that the great and terrible day of the Lord is near. That battle has not taken place. But before it does, Elijah will come to restore all things, just as Jesus said in Matthew 17. John was not Elijah — all things are not yet restored.

The prophets were merely instruments of God and often did not understand the prophecies themselves. The fact of two separate comings of the one Messiah was hidden from them. Yet they foretold that he would be suffering Savior as well as triumphant king and judge. His forerunners were described by both Malachi and Isaiah: two prophets, two forerunners, two comings.

It is quite likely that Elijah has been kept for the days described in Revelations 11:3-6. Here we are told of two witnesses. We do not know who these two will be, but their power as described in verse six is like that of Moses and Elijah. Some believe that these two will be Elijah and Enoch, neither of whom has experienced physical death as yet. For Elijah to be one of these is logical, since we are assured that he will be on earth as a forerunner of the Lord, and because the second coming of Christ is due soon after the death of these two witnesses.

In Jesus' day, some Jews believed that Jesus and John the Baptist were the same man, even though they were contemporaries! Jesus was very much aware of the errors of men.

In Matthew 16:13-17, Jesus asked his disciples,

> Who do men say that I, the Son of man, am? And they said, Some say thou art John the Baptist; some, Elijah; and others, Jeremiah, or one of the prophets. He saith unto them, But who say ye that I am? And Simon Peter answered and said, Thou art the Christ, the Son of the living God. And Jesus answered and said unto him,

> Blessed art thou, Simon Barjona; for flesh and blood hath not revealed it unto thee, but my Father, who is in heaven.

The guesses of the others were all wrong, but Jesus was happy that Simon Peter knew the right answer. The correct answer could only have been revealed to him by God. Many people, then as now, have not received this truth. We shouldn't be surprised to hear that some Jews believed in reincarnation.

Let's go back for just a moment to the Mount of Transfiguration, told in Matthew 17. Peter, James and John the Beloved were there. With their own eyes they saw Jesus transfigured and talking to two others. In verse four, Peter names these two others as Moses and Elijah. Judging by verse three, all three disciples knew who they were. Now, if Elijah and John the Baptist were the same man, would these three eyewitnesses not recognize him as John? After all, John had only recently died. They knew him very well. Some of the disciples of Jesus had even been disciples of John the Baptist first. Yet they knew this man to be Elijah, not John the Baptist.

Some would say that this person simply took his "best form" (as Elijah) for this appearance. But, even if it were the same man, his "best form" would be as John the Baptist. How do we know that? By looking at Christ's eulogy of John the Baptist: "Truly, of **all** men ever born, none shines more brightly than John the Baptist (Matthew 11:11 LB)." That "all" must include Elijah.

Besides John the Baptist and Elijah, there is another famous Bible pair I want to mention. These are Isaac's twin sons, Esau and Jacob. Their story is told in Genesis. Then Romans 9 beginning with verse 10 in *Good News for Modern Man* tells of them this way:

> For Rebecca's two sons had the same father, our ancestor

> Isaac. But in order that the choice of one son might be completely the result of God's own purpose, God said to her, 'The older will serve the younger.' He said this before they were born, before they had done anything either good or bad; so God's choice was based on His call, and not on anything they did. As the scripture says, 'I loved Jacob, but I hated Esau.' (Romans 9:10-13 TEV)

Reincarnationists take the past tense here in "loved" and "hated" to mean that these babies had lived before; and that God had prior cause to "love" or "hate" them.

But this passage emphatically does not mean that they had lived before. It even tells us that before they were born, they had done nothing either good or bad.

Neither does it mean that God accepted Jacob and rejected Esau on the basis of past experience.

It simply means that God is free to choose whomever he will to save, since he is the sovereign creator of all; and that he knew in advance how they would value spiritual things.

The past tense used in this verse, like many others, tends to confuse us since we attach so much importance to time. Time is vital to us, since our days are numbered; and because our whole lives must take time into account. "Timelessness" boggles our finite minds.

But time is not necessary to God. Past, present and future are alike to him. Like parade watchers, we see only a moment at a time, while God sees the whole parade at once.

God knew the future of these unborn babies, Jacob and Esau. Both were grandsons of Abraham, and eligible to carry out God's promises to him. Esau, the elder, thought so little of his heritage that he actually sold his birthright for a bowl of food. God knew that Esau would become the father of a heathen people, the Edomites. The Lord also knew that Jacob (who later became Israel) would train his family in spiritual things.

Malachi 1:2 and 3, where God says, "I loved Jacob and I hated Esau," is believed by many scholars to refer to the nations (descendants) of Jacob and Esau rather than the individuals. The nation of Israel is often called simply "Jacob," as Edom is sometimes called "Esau." The Book of Obadiah is an illustration of this.

Matthew Henry, the great Bible expositor, says,

> The choosing of Jacob the younger, and preferring him to Esau the older, were to intimate that the Jews, though the natural seed of Abraham, and the first-born of the church, should be laid aside; and the Gentiles, who were as the younger brother, should be taken in their stead, and have the birthright and blessing.[2]

Besides being real people, with real experiences, Jacob and Esau also serve as a "picture" which paints a spiritual truth. The original chosen people, the Jews (typified by elder Esau), should have received all the blessings of God. Because they rejected God's plan, these blessings were given instead to the true church (typified by younger Jacob).

After all, God sent the Messiah as promised, and the chosen people, the Jews, rejected him in spite of his impeccable credentials. With the exception of second coming prophecies, he fulfilled every single thing the prophets foretold of him. But most of the Jews chose their traditional ways rather than the true way.

John the Beloved says,

> But although he made the world, the world didn't recognize him when he came. Even in his own land and among his own people, the Jews, he was not accepted. Only a few would welcome and receive him. But to all who

> received him, he gave the right to become children of God. All they needed to do was to trust him to save them. All those who believe this are reborn! — not a physical rebirth resulting from human passion or plan — but from the will of God (John 1:10-13 LB).

Abraham was the grandfather of both Esau and Jacob. God's promises to Abraham (see Genesis 12:2 and 3) had to be fulfilled through the descendants of one of these boys. Abraham was justified by his faith in God, as was his younger grandson, Jacob; as is every person who trusts God. Every believer is a true descendant of Abraham, since they are of his spiritual lineage.

Paul clarifies the matter very well in Romans in his letter to the Roman believers, especially Romans 4:13-17:

> It is clear then, that God's promise to give the whole earth to Abraham and his descendants was not because Abraham obeyed God's laws but because he trusted God to keep his promise. So if you still claim that God's blessings go to those who are 'good enough,' then you are saying that God's promises to those who have faith are meaningless, and faith is foolish. But the fact of the matter is this: when we try to gain God's blessing and salvation by keeping his laws we always end up under his anger, for we always fail to keep them. The only way we can keep from breaking laws is not to have any to break!
>
> So God's blessings are given to us by faith, as a free gift; we are certain to get them whether or not we follow Jewish customs if we have faith like Abraham's, for Abraham is the father of us all when it comes to these matters of faith. That is what the Scriptures mean when they say that God made Abraham the father of many nations. God will accept all people in every nation who trust God as

> Abraham did. And this promise is from God himself, who makes the dead live again and speaks of future events with as much certainty as though they were already past (LB).

God knew that Jacob would have faith in him. And God loved Jacob even before he was born.

TWELVE

Remembered Lives, Deja Vu, Demons

Has it happened yet to you? You're having an ordinary conversation, or doing an ordinary chore. Suddenly you know exactly what will be said next, what will happen next. Or, you're in a place where you've never been before. Unexplainably, you know what you will see in the next room, around the corner, or out the window. You might be aware that certain pieces of furniture have been moved or taken away. Perhaps you will idly wonder when or why a doorway has been plastered over, only to realize with a start that you couldn't have known a door ever was there; but later you learn that there was.

There is a name for this: it is called deja vu. In French, it literally means "already seen." Webster's dictionary says, "In psychology, the illusion that one has previously had a given experience." Webster's doesn't say so, but it's spooky. It's tempting to try to fit this kind of experience into a past life, if it doesn't fit this one.

What about Bridey Murphy and other stories of "remembered" lives? An example: A small boy in India claimed to have been the owner of a large biscuit and soda shop in a neighboring city. He named names and places. He told how he, as a man, had become ill and died in a bathtub after eating too much curd. When taken to the city, the boy recognized places, people and changes made. He was right in nearly every detail. Convincing, isn't it?...and fully documented.[1]

Even more convincing to us are our own glimmers of remembered lives. I'll never forget the surprise with which I first heard the name of a famous American. Later, I became sure that my initial reaction was caused by recall of an acquaintance with him two hundred years ago. Sometimes it seems that our instincts fairly shout a previous knowledge of a person, place or thing. It seemed impossible to me that I could neither play the piano nor speak French. We all have experienced immediate like or dislike of certain people for no apparent reason.

Or how can we explain dreams like the one mentioned in the preface, insistent and clear, and seemingly trying to tell us something?

Fortune tellers and ouija boards are right very often. There are indeed many things going on all around us which make us wonder and marvel. Yes, it's true that strange things are happening. And they do have a common explanation.

It annoyed me to hear my pet theory, reincarnation, lumped together with occult subjects. But the connection is obvious to me now. St. Paul teaches us,

> For we wrestle not against flesh and blood, but against principalities, against powers, against the rulers of the darkness of this world (Ephesians 6:12).

What is he talking about? None other than the prince of this world, Satan; and his servants, "powers of the air," demons. The

Bible clearly teaches that demons have supernatural power, intelligence, knowledge and abilities. Only the power of God is greater than that of Satan. Without God's strength, we are utterly helpless against these powers. They can deceive, confuse, manipulate, direct us in any way they choose. They are quite able to control our emotions and thoughts, if we allow them to.

All of the strange things mentioned above can be traced to demonic activity. Dr. Merrill F. Unger, in his book, *Demons in the World Today,* cites biblical, physical, historical and existential evidence of demons.[2]

Dr. Unger clarifies the different forms of demonic activity. Demon possession is the actual physical indwelling of a human by a demon. Demon possession is rather rare: demon influence is not rare at all.

Dr. Unger says of demon **influence** that it

> may occur in different degrees of severity and in a variety of forms, both in Christians and non-Christians. In its less severe forms, demon attack comes from without through pressure, suggestion and temptation. When such pressure, suggestion and temptation are yielded to, the result is always an increased degree of demon influence. Although the human race fell in Adam and became prey to Satan and demons, the forces of darkness have always been severely restricted. They can enslave and oppress fallen man only to the degree he willingly violates the eternal moral law of God and exposes himself to evil.[3]

In the light of this, then, we can see that demon influence can be controlled by refusal to give in to pressure, suggestion and temptation. This is a tall order for sinful, weak humans —but divine help is available. Paul reveals that help in Philippians 4:13, "I can do all things through Christ, who strengtheneth me." Jesus has assured us that his power is greater than the power of Satan.

Of course, no power available to us is useful unless it is used. If we want protection, we must call upon the Lord. Otherwise, Satan and his demons are free to deceive us as they choose. They give us false impressions in order to turn us to other interests; anything, anything to swerve us from worshipping the Living God.

How do they deceive us? With lies! Jesus spoke very clearly to the Pharisees:

> Ye are of your father the devil, and the lusts of your father ye will do. He was a murderer from the beginning, and abode not in the truth, because there is no truth in him. When he speaketh a lie, he speaketh of his own; for he is a liar, and the father of it (John 8:44).

Since lies come so naturally to us, we know how best to lie. A lie is far more believable if it is partly true. Of course, the father of lies is the greatest expert of all. So, in the beginning of Satanic oppression, our interest is aroused by truths. A prediction comes true, a past event brought to light, it all seems so logical, right, and helpful. Sometimes just a little gets you hooked, sometimes it takes a lot. Anyone who does not know God's protection is helpless against these powers.

Another mighty weapon used against us is our feelings. Deja vu "feels" true. "There is a way that seemeth right unto a man, but the end thereof are the ways of death (Proverbs 14:12)." God carefully and clearly warns us over and over again not to lean to our own understanding (Proverbs 3:5). And with good reason. He made us, and he knows that our own understanding can be influenced by Satanic forces without our knowledge. Satan uses our own intelligence to trip us.

There are several reasons why people get tricked into

holding occult beliefs, and they themselves are ultimately responsible. These reasons include:

* They want to uncover hidden knowledge.

* They want to know the future.

* They want to exercise supernatural powers.

These all have their roots in pride. These powers would seem to elevate them above other people. No matter if they protest that they want these powers to help others; the pride factor still is there.

God's word gives all needed information, but learning it takes work. How much easier to just (directly or indirectly) ask Satan for it. After all, Satan's ways can provide some true information, and we do seem to get these three choice goodies —lots of times. If you are determined to know, and God won't tell you, you must obviously turn to other means. This is what King Saul did at Endor. What he learned was true, but learning it was a great mistake (1 Chronicles 10:13-14).

The Bible says,

> "So why are you trying to find out the future by consulting witches and mediums? Don't listen to their whisperings and mutterings. Can the living find out the future from the dead? Why not ask your God? 'Check these witches' words against the Word of God!' he says. 'If their messages are different than mine, it is because I have not sent them; for they have no light or truth in them. My people will be led away captive, stumbling, weary and hungry. And because they are hungry they will rave and shake their fists at heaven and curse their King and their God. Wherever they look there will be trouble and anguish and dark despair. And they will be thrust out into the darkness' " (Isaiah 8:19-20 LB).

That's a high price to pay for imperfect knowledge. Working through witches and mediums, plus ouija boards, etc., demons get half-truths and complete lies to the willing and eager listener.

It matters not whether a demon is physically in us or merely influencing us; deceiving us is a simple matter. This explains deja vu, seemingly impossible memories and dreams like the one mentioned in the preface. (Now I understand why I never dreamed that dream again once I had accepted reincarnation —its purpose was accomplished!) These deceptions also explain God's insistence throughout the Bible that we avoid astrology, mediums, fortune-tellers, witchcraft — the whole occult world.

In Genesis 3:5, Satan tempted Eve by telling her, "Your eyes shall be opened, and ye shall be as gods." That sounded great to Eve, and it sounds great to us. The search for special knowledge goes on. How tempting it is to turn to occult sources rather than the word of God! In 1 Kings 22:22, God permits a lying spirit to speak through false prophets. This is not unfair of God, for if we turn to false prophets instead of the Living God, he has warned us, and lies are all we can rightfully expect.

God says,

> Do not defile yourselves by consulting mediums or wizards, for I am Jehovah your God (Leviticus 19:31 LB).
>
> I will set my face against anyone who consults mediums or wizards instead of me and I will cut that person off from his people (Leviticus 20:6 LB).
>
> A medium or a wizard — whether man or woman —shall surely be stoned to death. They have caused their own doom (Leviticus 20:27 LB).
>
> There shall not be found among you anyone who makes his son or daughter pass through the fire, or that uses

> divination, or an observer of clouds, or a fortune-teller, or a witch, or a charmer [hypnotist], or one who asks of familiar spirits, or a wizard, or one who calls to the dead (Deuteronomy 18:10-11 KJV).

Why is God so adamant about this? Because we are so easily fooled, and all we will get from these are lies, destruction and hell. God does not want us to perish.

Oh, you say, but what the medium or the Ouija board said was **true!** What Jesus said was true, too — let's get excited about that instead! You say, well, this message was more personal. What? More personal than the Son of God taking each one of our individual sins upon himself and voluntarily taking the punishment we deserved? How can it get more personal than that?

Just read what Jesus said, and each time the text says "you" or "any man," etc., substitute your name. What a beautifully simple way to illustrate the very personal love of God!

God does love us; but be assured also that neither Satan nor his aides, demons, do. Their underlying motive is always our ultimate destruction. They know God, and don't even love **him!**

> Are there still some among you who hold that 'only believing' is enough? Believing in one God? Well, remember that demons believe this too — so strongly that they tremble in terror (James 2:19 LB).

The demons know him. Does that surprise you? In the Bible, we are told of several encounters Jesus had with demon-possessed people. Without exception, these demons knew him. Even though they knew him, they had not accepted him, and so were not saved. Besides this, they have knowledge — we can have faith. "For we walk by faith, not by sight (2 Corinthians 5:7)." The demons have seen him and are unable to have faith.

Even so, when we see him, all chances for faith will be past. We will know by sight, not faith.

> Blessed and happy and to be envied are those who have never seen Me, and yet have believed and adhered to and trusted in and relied on Me (John 20:29 ANT).

It is intriguing to realize that demons may know us, too (See Acts 19:15).

Consider a newborn puppy or kitten. Think of the relationship between yourself and the newborn animal. It is blind, helpless and totally unable to comprehend you, or your ways or your power over it. You can decide whether to keep it, give it away or sell it, and to whom. For any one of a hundred different reasons, you may even decide to destroy it. You have all the power, and this helpless creature doesn't even know it. This is exactly our condition before demons without God's protection.

Do you believe you have lived before? A demon has found a way to convince you; by oppression, lies, influence, or perhaps even possession. Do you believe in magic or astrology? You're right; they have plenty of power. Do you know a medium or someone whose predictions come true? I don't doubt it for a moment. Watch out, God does not work in these ways. It comes not from him, but from the "powers of darkness, powers of the air." God has warned us about these things for our own good. Jesus said himself that Satan is the father of lies. Satan is willing to show you wonderful things and even give you temporary powers. But the lie will always destroy, and the king of liars has no honor, no loyalty. He simply seeks to devour.

But, you may say, what about remembered lives? In the beginning of this chapter, I told the true story of an Indian boy whose amazing experience certainly seems to prove reincarnation. Well, you're right, after a fashion. I believe it does prove reincarnation, of a kind. Since the Bible makes it abundantly clear that it is appointed unto (hu)man(s) once to die, and after that the judgment (Hebrews 9:27), then it can't be the soul which is reincarnated. But something else can be. And that something is an indwelling demon. In the case of the boy, I believe the evidence proves he was simply indwelt by the same demonic force which had previously possessed a business man. The demon, as virtually a part of the man, naturally knew all about him, including his secrets. How could it not? Speaking through the boy was easy. Demons do it often through mediums. Their impersonations of the dead are very effective, too.

A couple I know personally were convinced of reincarnation because, although they spoke no French, their toddler spoke French rather than English. Occult believers whom the mother knew assured her that the girl had been French in the last life; that as she got older those memories would fade out. When the child was ten, many demons were cast out of her. One of these insisted that it didn't have to leave the girl since it had been there since she was born. It said it had indwelt a French person the last time. The puzzle suddenly fit together. The mother had opened herself to many occult subjects, even while carrying the child. This fascinating true story is told in *Out! In the Name of Jesus!*, by Pat Brooks.[4]

In the same way that Satan can use the mother's body to infect unborn babies with drug addiction or AIDS, innocent children are exposed to demon possession through parental occult involvement.

In one documented case after another, it has been proven that demon possession can be real; and that the demons can truly leave one body for another. Missionaries in lands where there is little restraining Christian influence tell frightening stories about such cases.

Ian Stevenson's book, *Twenty Cases Suggestive of Reincarnation*,[5] is much less mysterious when read with demonic power in mind. In these cases, demonic activity seems obvious. Dr. Stevenson says that he can conceive of at least eight alternative explanations to all of the cases he has researched, and points out that none of the cases actually prove reincarnation (of souls).

In *Occult Bondage and Deliverance*, Kurt Koch gives case histories, too, with an understanding of the demon workings in them.[6] He cautions against the wrong diagnosis of demon possession. Actual possession is rather rare. More often, the victim's problems stem from demon influence, subjection, oppression or mental illness. More often yet, we have ourselves to blame for our sinful behavior.

But possession is spreading in our day because so many people are innocently opening their minds. Under the guise of regression to hunt for former identities, Satan has persuaded thousands to undergo hypnotism. Whether it's called hypnotism, ESP, relaxation therapy, Scientology, regression, transcendental meditation, trance channelling, or anything else, a clearing of the mind invites demonic control. Once they get control, they show no mercy, but can literally make the victim believe anything.

The Bible speaks of the "powers of the air" in Ephesians 2. Anytime we invite other powers into our mind, we are actually asking the "powers of the air" to enter. Since Satan is the prince of this world, his demons have "the run of the place;" they are the powers of the air. Readily available, eager to take possession of any human mind, all they need is that open invitation. The invitation is issued in the quiet of the seance, in the seeking of mystical healing outside the Holy Spirit, in the use of Ouija boards, astrology, witchcraft, fortune telling, hypnotism, card layings, spiritism, trances, sexual sins, illicit drugs, study of falsehoods of any kind, and, of course, heathen religions.

These are only some of the ways demons can gain possession of a human being. There are many others.

Demons also have special claims to people whose parents or grandparents (or other close relatives) were involved in the occult. We see this throughout the Bible. For instance, in Exodus 20 where the Ten Commandments were given, God names first the sin of bowing down to other gods. He warns that he is "a jealous God, visiting the iniquity of the fathers upon the children unto the third and fourth generation of them that hate me (Exodus 20:5)." People who bow down to false gods teach their children to do the same, whether or not they consciously do.

What the parents do affects the children enormously. Even though they have free will, children can be spiritually blinded by Satan for their whole lifetime because of demonic control of their forebears. Even in the natural realm, consider the lifelong damage done by abusive adults, or simply dysfunctional families. Psychological scars in adults often reappear in their offspring unless the healing power of Jesus Christ intervenes. By the same token, those who worship the "True and Living God" pass his blessings on to their descendants. Psalm 102:28 says, "But our families will continue; generation after generation will be preserved by your protection (LB)."

Occasionally, demons can indwell animals also. At the beginning of the fifth chapter of the Gospel according to Mark, Jesus met a demon-possessed mad man. You would do well to read this account very carefully. Jesus gave the demons permission to enter a herd of swine which immediately ran violently down a steep place and were drowned in the sea. One of the most startling aspects of this account is that the swine numbered about two thousand! All of them went berserk from demon possession and all of the demons had been housed in this one unfortunate man. No wonder no one could tame him!

> To the reality and personality of demons the New Testament (NT) Scriptures bear abundant testimony. As to their origin, nothing is clearly revealed, but they are not to be confounded with the angels mentioned in 2 Peter 2:4, Jude 6. Summary: (1) Demons are spirits (Matthew 12:43-45), Satan's emissaries (Matthew 12:26-27), and so numerous as to make Satan's power practically ubiquitous (Mark 5:9). (2) They are capable of entering and controlling both men and beasts (Mark 5:2-5, 11-13), and earnestly seek embodiment, without which, apparently, they are powerless for evil (Matthew 12:43-44, Mark 5:10-12). (3) Demon influence and demon possession are discriminated in the NT. Instances of the latter are Matthew 4:24; 8:16,28 33; 9:32; 12:22; Mark 1:32; 5:15-16, 18; Luke 8:36... (4) Demons are unclean, sullen, violent and malicious (Matthew 8:28; 9:33; 10:1; 12:43)... (5) They know Jesus as Most High God and recognize His supreme authority (Matthew 8:31-32; Mark 1:23-24; Acts 19:15; James 2:19). (6) They know their eternal fate to be one of torment (Matthew 8:29; Luke 8:31). (7) They inflict physical maladies (Matthew 12:22; 17:15-18; Luke 13:16). However, mental disease is to be distinguished from the disorder of mind due to demoniacal control. (8) Demon influence may manifest itself in religious asceticism (1 Timothy 4:1-3), degenerating unto uncleanness. (9) The sign of demon influence in religion is departure from the faith; i.e., the body of revealed truth in the scriptures (1 Timothy 4:1). (10) The demons maintain a conflict with

> Christians who would be spiritual (Ephesians 6:12; 1 Timothy 4:1-3). The Christians' resources are prayer and bodily control (Matthew 17:20), 'the whole armor of God' (Ephesians 6:13-18). (11) All unbelievers are open to demon possession (Ephesians 2:2). (12) Exorcism in the name of Jesus Christ (Acts 16:18) was practiced for demon possession. And, (13) one of the awful features of the apocalyptic judgments in which this age will end is an emergence of demons out of the abyss (Revelations 9:1-11,20).[7]

What about true believers in Christ, born not only of the flesh, but also of spirit? True believers are indwelt by the Holy Spirit. Can even they be indwelt by demons?

> Now the Spirit speaketh expressly that, in the latter times, some shall depart from the faith, giving heed to seducing spirits, and doctrines of devils (1 Timothy 4:1).

This obviously means that these people once had true faith, but turned away. This is repeated in 2 Timothy 4:4, "And they shall turn away their ears from the truth, and shall be turned unto fables." Now, having turned away from the truth, what is left to them but untruth? "Fables" and lies must come from the father and lover of lies, Satan. The Holy Spirit guides only to the truth. Naturally, even a true believer who gives heed to seducing spirits and lies has opened himself to powers other than the Holy Spirit.

For example, consider Ananias and Sapphira spoken of in Acts 5. They were part of the church of Jerusalem. Acts 4:32-37 could be interpreted to either include or exclude this couple from "those that believed." In either case, Peter asked why Satan had filled their heart to lie to the Holy Spirit. In his own heart, Ananias had conceived the idea of the lie, then Satan had been allowed to follow through and consume both man and wife with it. The church did not pray for their deliverance; both man and wife were struck dead.

In another instance alluded to by Paul, a member of the Corinthian church was deep in sin. Paul urged them in the strongest terms to exclude him from their membership. He wrote:

> You are to hand this man over to Satan for his body to be destroyed, so that his spirit may be saved in the Day of the Lord (1 Corinthians 5:5 TEV).

Since immorality is often a sign of demonic activity, it is possible that both of these cases deal with the demonic possession of believers. This is not to say that in such cases they lost their salvation, for Jesus promises that he will never leave us nor forsake us. Many sinful children of God die before their time, lest they sin further and bring dishonor to their heavenly Father. This is also substantiated by Paul's statement that because some believers were taking communion in an unworthy way, "many of you are weak and sick, and some have even died (1 Corinthians 11:30 LB)."

If it is possible for a true believer to open up to demonic activity, then we can see how serious a matter this is: rather than deliverance, some die.

In Acts 19:18, it was **believers** who gathered to burn their own occult books and charms, valued together at about $10,000. Although I didn't know why, one of the first things I did after my conversion was to cancel membership in an occult book club, and then to destroy all my books on reincarnation, etc. I only knew I didn't want them around any more. Months later, I saw a new Christian publicly burn cartons of occult books. Like me, she didn't want anyone else to be misled by them.

By religious errors, occult involvement, deliberate sins, Satanic "inheritance," idolatry, atheism, rejection of Jesus, and other means, demons can gain **legal access** to our minds. No person should have any traffic, however small, with any of these. From astrology to Zen, all are Satan's territory. The unsaved are especially vulnerable to Satan through these means; but not even Christians are immune if they are foolish enough to expose themselves to the enemy.

Generally speaking, three questions can be asked to determine whether demonic influence is present. Is there some kind of enslavement? Is there torment? Is the life defiled or contaminated? All or any of these could be strong indication of demonic activity.

Can a Christian have a demon? This is a good question that is admirably answered in Don Basham's book with the same title.[8]

Bible believing theologians are divided on the issue. Some claim that no evil spirit could indwell a body also inhabited by the Holy Spirit of God. They believe that demon possessed people who claim to be Christians were never truly born again.

Others believe that being "born of the Spirit" and being "filled with the Spirit" are vastly different levels of spiritual maturity and that it is due to this difference that some believers can be demon possessed, while more mature believers cannot. Theologians who hold to this view usually believe that Christians can be **still** possessed (from before their salvation), or **become** possessed afterward through deliberate sins, particularly occult involvement. When believers walk in obedience to the Word of God, Satan can not enter in. But wherever Satan is invited, he will go. This illustrates the crucial issue of knowing God's Word and being obedient to it.

Dr. Kurt Koch cites several cases of possession of true believers in *Occult Bondage and Deliverance*.[9] One of these was a missionary positive that it could not happen, until it happened to him personally.

Hal Lindsey also quotes cases supporting this view.[10] So does Dr. Merrill Unger. He says,

> Believers can be hindered, bound and oppressed by Satan and even indwelt by one or more demons, who may derange the mind and afflict the body....The writer during many years of pastoral ministry and counseling has witnessed the grip Satan can hold over truly regenerated believers. He has often noted that some believers are delivered from evil spirits when they are saved, others are not, and must be delivered later by fasting and prayer. Others struggle on in the Christian life, never completely set free from demon power.[11]

Dr. Unger also quotes Hobart E. Freeman, a pastor, as saying,

'In my personal experience, the majority of those for whom I have prayed for deliverance from occult oppression or subjection were Christians, including ministers and the wives of ministers.'[12]

Dr. Unger goes on later to stress the responsibility of spiritual leaders to see that deliverance is made available to those who need it.

Satan's efforts to make hypnotism respectable are paying huge dividends to him and his demonic forces. Many people, including Christians, see no connection between hypnotism and the occult.

The many fakes and failures of spiritism merely serve to cover the fact that spiritist mediums actually do contact spirits, and these are always evil spirits. The one and only condition which a medium must meet in order to contact the spirits is complete passivity. Body and brain must be completely out of the control of the medium. All faculties and will must be "let go." This is a perfect description of the hypnotized state. It is completely and diametrically opposed to God's methods.

According to Jessie Penn-Lewis:

> By dismissing these things as 'nothing,' we have missed understanding the **law** by which these evil spirits work. There is not one sentence in Paul's Epistles where he tells you to become 'passive.' Every time he speaks of the Holy Spirit there is a reference to activity on the part of the believer. 'I **labour**, striving according to His working (Colossians 1:29).' God works 'according to law,' and the law for the working of the Holy Spirit is **'active cooperation.'** The law for the working of evil spirits is **'passive submission.'** God desires 'fellow workers with Him:' evil spirits want to **use you** as a passive instrument.[13]

In January 1975, a story appeared across America of a minister in Virginia who had hypnotized his wife. Under a trance, she began to speak German, a language she had never learned. Since she was in a trance, she did not cooperate in speaking at all, or have any later recollection of it. She told of a German life years ago. These people say they do not believe in reincarnation, but are at a loss to explain the phenomena. This may be a case of a believer deliberately entering enemy territory and becoming possessed as a result.[14]

Christians willing to draw closer to God often have spontaneous deliverances. In one case an elderly lady had hated a relative since childhood, with good reason. As she sought a closer walk with the Lord, she "felt the hatred drawn up and out," and she was able to truly forgive that person in her heart. In another case, a minister was kneeling at the altar during communion: he said "I felt something leave me," and anxiety over a broken friendship was lifted. In still another case, a woman kneeling in prayer confessed idolatry, since for years she had put her husband in God's rightful place. She says she stopped her prayer in amazement, asking "What was that?" as she felt something "pulled out of me and away." Again, a Christian found that very often as the Lord Jesus Christ received praise, deliverance followed. These lives have been changed and healed.

In none of the above cases did the Christian realize what had happened. Demon possession was not considered, since it seems impossible in this modern age. All they knew was that something evil actually left, and that their lives were better for it. But in each case it took confession, prayer, praise, forgiveness, trust, faith and/or fasting to bring deliverance **after** salvation.

No deliverance should ever be attempted without the presence of two or more mature born-again Christians who are familiar with spiritual warfare, and who are willing to pray, fast and sacrifice in many ways to do battle. The possessed person must confess Jesus as personal Savior. He or she must be willing to renounce and turn from all occult involvement, and to get rid of all of Satan's items like Ouija boards, tarot cards, occult books, astrological symbols, etc. This person's commitment to Christ must be real, and the willingness to be filled instead with the Holy Spirit must also be genuine. He or she must be truly willing to forgive the wrongs anyone has done to them. All sins must be confessed to God (not necessarily to men); and the believer, the house, the families of all concerned must be protected and covered by the blood of Jesus. All this preparation is vital. Satan will use any kind of loophole as an in-road. The person delivered must be carefully instructed against becoming possessed again.

I recommend especially *Satan is Alive and Well...*[15], *Demons in the World Today,*[16] and Robertson's book *Answers...* [17] for further information on this last point.

As we read the Gospels, it is amazing how much of Jesus' ministry dealt with casting out of demons. These took many forms; but they always recognized him, acknowledged him as God, and feared him. They fear his name even today. When the name of Jesus Christ is used against a demon, and it is commanded out in that name by a mature born again Christian, that demon has no choice. It **must** leave.

However, disaster awaits any unsaved person trying to use Jesus' name in exorcism. See Acts 19:13-17.

In the New Testament, both the apostles and ordinary disciples were given the power to cast out demons (Acts 8:7; Luke 10:17). Before Jesus ascended into heaven, he gave a listing of signs that would follow those that believe; casting out demons is one of those signs (Mark 16:17). His ascension marked the beginning of the "Church Age," which will not end until his return. The power to cast out demons **still** is one of the privileges of certain believers as the Holy Spirit wills (1 Corinthians 12:11, Luke 10:19). Some can cast out demons, some cannot. (In the same way, some have the gift of healing, most do not.)

Friends of mine who have a deliverance ministry say that they never cast demons out of an unsaved person. This is because Jesus warned against doing this and explained very clearly why:

> For when Satan, strong and fully armed, guards his palace, it is safe — until someone stronger and better-armed attacks and overcomes him and strips him of his weapons and carries off his belongings. Anyone who is not for me is against me; if he isn't helping me, he is hurting my cause. When a demon is cast out of a man, it goes to the deserts, searching there for rest; but finding none, it returns to the person it left, and finds that its former home is all

> swept and clean. Then it goes and gets seven other demons more evil than itself, and they all enter the man. And so the poor fellow is seven times worse off than he was before (Luke 11:21-26 LB).

It is a tragic mistake to cast out a demon without filling that "empty place" with the Holy Spirit!

These friends, in explaining this to me, reminded me of the scriptural teaching that there is a true warfare going on — the battle between the forces of God and the forces of Satan. Just like any warfare, victories can be temporary. Ground lost must be either safeguarded by the new owner or retaken by the enemy. When, therefore, a demon is cast out, the area of life and body it controlled must be claimed and filled with the Holy Spirit. An unsaved person **has** no Holy Spirit. The demon which has left this person will return to find the place empty, and will bring others back with it.

Not all of our sins are demon inspired. Let's not look for demons under every bush and hangnail. The world around us and our own sinful flesh are part of the problem of sin.

A listing of sins which we do, even without demon possession, is given in Galatians 5:19-21:

> What human nature does is quite plain. It shows itself in immoral, filthy, and indecent actions; in worship of idols and witchcraft. People become enemies, they fight, become jealous, angry, and ambitious. They separate into parties and groups; they are envious, get drunk, have orgies, and do other things like these. I warn you now as I have before: those who do these things will not receive the Kingdom of God (TEV).

Then the very next verse goes on to contrast the evidence of the Holy Spirit:

> But the Spirit produces love, joy, peace, patience, kindness, goodness, faithfulness, humility, and self-control. There is no law against such things as these. And those who belong to Christ Jesus have put to death their human nature, with all its passions and desires. The Spirit has given us life; he must also control our lives. We must not be proud, or irritate one another, or be jealous of one another.

Even in discussing the matter of demons, there is danger. C. S. Lewis has said that there are two methods Satan uses against us.[18] They are: (1) to get you to ignore the demonic, or, failing that, (2) to get you obsessed with it.

It's wise to remember that the Bible does not make too great a fuss about demons. It acknowledges their existence, tells how to get rid of them, reveals whose servants they are, and certain traits they have, etc., but over all, the Bible does not show a great interest in demons. This is a healthy outlook for us.

In ancient Babylon, the people lived in constant fear, because they believed that demons were everywhere and in everything. It is interesting to note that as the Babylonian religion (see chapter 20) now gains popularity again, so does dread of demons and obsession with possession and exorcism.

Rather than dwell on demons, the Bible emphasizes Christ. Also, the Bible says,

> Finally, brethren, whatever things are true, whatever things are honest, whatever things are just, whatever things are pure, whatever things are lovely, whatever things are of good report; if there be any virtue, and if there be any praise, think on these things (Philippians 4:8).

We must be on guard, however, not to give the devil a foothold. If someone deliberately rebels against God they are very foolish. To persist in this rebellion is to compound the foolishness and invite real trouble. If we really love God and seek to do his will, he will protect us, but we must obey him and sever all ties to his enemy.

The Bible clearly teaches that it is the shed blood of Jesus which offers remission of sins; "without shedding of blood there is no remission (Hebrews 9:22)." When a true child of God claims the blood of Jesus for forgiveness of sins and protection against demons; they will flee away — they can't stand against it. Revelation 12:10-11 tells of Satan, who accuses us before God, and of the Christians who overcame him. How did they overcome Satan? "And they overcame him by the blood of the Lamb, and by the word of their testimony (Revelation 12:11)."

The power of demons is real; but more powerful still is the only remedy: Jesus Christ.

THIRTEEN

Satan, Witchcraft

Someone wants you to believe in reincarnation: Satan.

The last thing I want to do is to give any glory to Satan, but it is important that we recognize that he exists, that he is to be contended with, and that he does have plenty of power.

Until a few years ago, it seemed almost impossible to find an American who could take Satan seriously. The joker with horns and tail is funny. But Satan is far from funny. Peter tells us,

> Be sober, be vigilant, because your adversary, the devil, like a roaring lion walketh about, seeking whom he may devour (1 Peter 5:8).

Some joke! Satan uses many sinister tactics.

In Ezekiel 28 a man, "the **prince** of Tyre" is rebuked by God because, "thou hast said, I am a god (Ezekiel 28:2,9)." His destruction is foretold. Then the real power behind that foolish prince is addressed as the "**king** of Tyre" (vs 12). The "king of Tyre," the occult true ruler of that nation, could only be Satan. The Bible reveals here Satan's glorious past, his casting out of heaven and his future destruction. Even his presence in Eden is noted. Eve and the "prince of Tyre" had believed the same lie —they would be gods. (Genesis 3:5)

Satan's formula is the same one he initiated with Eve in Genesis 3:1-4.

(1) He questions God's Word. (Hath God said? vs.1)

(2) He contradicts God's Word. (Ye shall not die. vs. 4)

(3) He attacks God's character. (Maligning his motives. vs. 5)

(4) He lies about the benefits of sin. (Ye shall be as gods. vs. 5.)

Ever the counterfeit of God, Satan uses many names. While God's names reveal holy aspects of his character, Satan's names are meant to obscure his identity. Satan was at first Lucifer, "son of the morning." He was originally a beautiful, wise and anointed citizen of heaven until iniquity was found in him. (Ezekiel 28:15)

The only Biblical occurrence of the name "Lucifer" is in Isaiah 14:12. There it says, "How art thou fallen from heaven, O Lucifer, son of the morning! How art thou cut down to the ground, who didst weaken the nations!" Then are named the five "I will" statements which Lucifer made to cause his downfall. These related his prideful desire to be worshipped as God, and constituted the true original sin. Modern Luciferians deny that they worship Satan, but openly call him the "son of the morning," the title which clearly pinpoints him as the originator of the ongoing rebellion against God.

An eyewitness to Lucifer's fall from heaven was Jesus Christ of Nazareth. Hearing his disciples rejoicing that even the demons were subject to them, Jesus testified,

> I beheld Satan as lightning fall from heaven. Behold I give unto you power to tread on serpents and scorpions,

> and over all the power of the enemy; and nothing shall by any means hurt you (Luke 10:18).

Jesus thus (1) showed that demons and Satan were of the same power, (2) that he saw the fall from heaven, (3) that he who fell, Lucifer (Isaiah 14:12), was now named Satan, (4) that evil was linked to Satan, and (5) that the disciples of Jesus had power over God's enemy, Satan, and his whole realm.

In Revelation 12:9 other names of Satan are used in describing a war in heaven:

> And the great dragon was cast out, that old serpent, called the Devil and Satan, who deceiveth the whole world; he was cast out into the earth, and his angels were cast out with him.

Satan had a plan to overthrow God and to take over the kingdom of heaven.

> How art thou fallen from heaven, O Lucifer, son of the morning! How art thou cut down to the ground, who didst weaken the nations! For thou hast said in thine heart, I will ascend into heaven, I will exalt my throne above the stars of God; I will sit also upon the mount of the congregation, in the sides of the north, I will ascend above the heights of the clouds, I will be like the Most High (Isaiah 14:12-14).

The fact that these plans were thwarted and the planner thrown out of heaven in defeat discloses the basis of Satan's hatred for God. He wished to destroy God, but could the Creator succumb to the creature? This is the theme of many horror stories —that the "monster" turns on the "professor" and destroys him. We recognize the true horror of such a happening. But, in actuality, God the creator has total power over Satan. Satan has power only as God allows. Satan's desire has never changed. He has always wanted to be worshipped instead of

God. He knows any worship he receives is only temporary; that in the end every knee shall bow to God and every tongue shall confess that **He** is God (Romans 14:11). This does infuriate Satan. Since he has no power to wound God personally, he has devised another way. Just like an earthly war, when one side has all the power, the enemy must resort to guerrilla warfare and is limited to wounding rather than defeating those he hates. This is what Satan is doing. He cannot defeat God, and so he causes him great pain. This is easily accomplished by luring us to our doom. God loves us so much that he is not willing that **any** should perish.

> For God so loved the world that he gave his only begotten Son, that whosoever believeth in him should not perish, but have everlasting life (John 3:16).

We are all precious to God. He is truly grieved each time one is lost. This is the first reason that Satan wants us to be damned.

The second is that Christ has promised to come again. Then Satan's power will be ended, and eventually he and his servants will be cast into the lake of everlasting fire (Revelation 20). Satan is fighting for time! The longer he can delay the completion of the true church, the longer it will be before Jesus will return. This is one reason all true Christians must do everything possible to be conformed to God's image and to win souls for Christ — it will hasten the time of his return and the end of Satan's power. See also Isaiah 14:15-17.

Reincarnation is just another angle on Satan's lie of salvation by works. This explains why Satan's servants, witches, believe in reincarnation. At the time I accepted the teaching of reincarnation, I did not know that it was one of the basic tenets of witchcraft. If I had, I would not have been such an easy prey, for I knew that the scriptures tell of God's hatred for witchcraft. How can a God of love hate? Because these are the ways that

Satan uses to cause our destruction. God does not want us destroyed.

It seems so frustrating! If God does not want us destroyed, why does he allow Satan any power?[1] Why doesn't he put an end to him now?

The Bible gives the answer.

The Living Bible paraphrases Peter's words this way:

> But don't forget this, dear friends, that a day or a thousand years from now is like tomorrow to the Lord. He isn't really being slow about his promised return, even though it sometimes seems that way. But he is waiting, for the good reason that he is not willing that any should perish, and he is giving more time for sinners to repent (2 Peter 3:8-9).

God does not want puppets who **must** love him. That's why he gave us free will. He wants to call out from among us a people who would **choose** to love him —choose of our own free will to live our lives and give our hearts to him. Every day more humans make the choice to love God. The Bible says that there is rejoicing in heaven over every sinner who repents and turns to Christ with true faith. By choosing good over evil, we become strong.

It is vital for us to realize that even though he is already defeated at Calvary (Colossians 2:15), Satan has some temporary comfort in several respects: (1) he is the acknowledged "prince of this world (John 14:30)," (2) he is causing the destruction of many, to the pain of God, (3) he is now the "prince of devils (Matthew 12:24)," (4) he is now receiving worship also from human beings, both knowingly and unknowingly, and (5) being now the "god of this world" (2 Corinthians 4:4).

As previously mentioned, worship is what Satan has always

wanted. Since the beginning of sin in the world, he has been receiving worship. Unknowingly, many people are giving worship to Satan in many different ways. Satan is far too clever to make it obvious to most people where their worship is directed. He doesn't announce himself, as a rule. Rather, he influences them to put anything at all before God, often using phony names.

Exodus 20:3 gives the first commandment: "Thou shalt have no other gods before me." Make no mistake, whatever is first in our thoughts and hearts is our god. It may be a denomination, or a spouse or child, or a way of life, or our own self and selfish desires; it may be money or it may be false beliefs of any kind. Whatever is first is our religion.

All false religions are truly Satan worship. God's way is truth: any religion opposed to truth is against God and reaches Satan. Demons and their master love religion — any religion as long as it is not God's.

This is illustrated by an Old Testament name for Satan: Baal. For instance, Judges 2:11 says, "And the children of Israel did evil in the sight of the Lord, and served Baalim." Baalim is a plural term for heathen gods and idols, consolidated and denounced by God as the worship of Baal.

The many Bible names given for Satan reveal the truth that worship of any god but God is actually the worship of Satan. For instance, Satan was called Baal, Baalim, Baal-zebub, Beel'zebub, Bel, Belial, Abaddon, Apollyon, the devil, the prince of this world, the god of this world. If the true and living God is not worshipped, the god of this world is. All false gods and all false religions have one root: Satan.

When King Ahaziah, King of Israel, was ill, he sent messengers to Ekron to the temple of the god Baal-zebub to ask whether he would recover. But God rebuked the king through

Elijah the prophet for inquiring of Baal-zebub, and he died. He had sought the same god, Baal, as his forefathers (2 Kings 1:1-4).

Then in Luke, we are told how Jesus used the names of Satan and Beel'zebub interchangeably. Jesus was casting out demons, but the Pharisees doubted the source of his power.

> Some of them said, He casteth out demons through Beel'zebub, the chief of the demons. And others testing him, sought of him a sign from heaven. But he, knowing their thoughts, said unto them, Every kingdom divided against itself is brought to desolation; and a house divided against a house falleth. If Satan also be divided against himself, how shall his kingdom stand? Because ye say that I cast out demons through Beel'zebub (Luke 11:15-18).

Satan is Baal, Baal is Satan. God calls the worship of Baal harlotry. God's people are to love him first and foremost, but how many times we are told that they "went a-whoring after other gods! (Jeremiah 3:1-5)" In 2 Kings 17:16-17 we are told how the Israelites behaved:

> And they left all the commandments of the Lord their God, and made them melted images, even two calves, and made an idol, and worshipped all the host of heaven [astrology] and served Baal. And they caused their sons and daughters to pass through the fire, and used divination and enchantments, and sold themselves to do evil in the sight of the Lord, to provoke him to anger.

This same chapter relates that many people learned to worship the Lord, but they also worshipped other gods, ignoring God's command: Never worship other gods (2 Kings 17:41).

The specific worship of Baal involved tremendous cruelty, particularly to helpless children. This is evident today among those who openly worship Satan: it is a poorly kept secret.

Another secret which is being exposed in our time is the widespread worship of Lucifer under the mask of Freemasonry. Masonic initiates are not told where their worship is actually directed until it's too late to back out. Beautiful rainbow imagery is liberally used. (See chapter 13 Recommended Reading.) Other groups secretly worshipping Lucifer (Satan) are being exposed, too. Check your local Christian bookstore.

Manasseh was King of Judah, and he worshipped Baal:

> He [Manasseh] built altars for Baal and made a shameful Asherah idol, just as Ahab the King of Israel had done. Heathen altars to the sun god, moon god, and the gods of the stars were even placed in the Temple of the Lord — in the very city and building which the Lord had selected to honor his own name. And he sacrificed one of his sons as a burnt offering on a heathen altar. He practiced black magic and used fortune-telling, and patronized mediums and wizards. So the Lord was very angry for Manasseh was an evil man. (2 Kings 21:3-6 LB).

Diverting worship away from God and (even indirectly) to himself is the main goal of Satan.

What would be the logical ways to accomplish this main goal? If you were Satan, what strategy would you follow?

First: Make people think that you don't really exist. Their blindness would make possible all kinds of manipulation. Revel in worship directed your way through false religions. Hide your power and almost never show it openly.

Second: If they vaguely suspect that you exist, then plant a comical image of yourself in their minds, like a tail, pitchfork, toothy grin, so that they will laugh rather than take you seriously. Continue to use your power undercover.

Third: Disguise yourself as an "angel of light," and have your ministers do the same. Have them preach "good works" and "being nice," tell the people to get involved in social action, let them shout for "brotherly love." See to it, if possible, that the deceived call themselves "Christians;" let them destroy the meaning of the name by living for self instead of Christ. See that they join churches and, even unknowingly work from within to destroy the truth. Never let them be exposed to the gospel, but keep them frantically busy with "church work." Keep them puffed up with pride and let others see them as hypocrites. Let them use the Bible, but only with your supervision; let them ever learn, but never come to a knowledge of the truth. Infiltrate the seminaries with unbelieving professors. Make sure that graduates have less faith than when they entered the seminary. Use your power to give most of the people in this category worldly rewards. Since you are the prince of this world, let some of them have riches, power, fame; it will only last a few years anyway. Let them have general peace of mind: hide from them their fear of death. Make sure that some of your people have sunk so low in obvious sin that the majority of the deceived ones will contrast themselves and come up smelling like roses. If someone tells them the gospel, make them ignore it, laugh at it, or better yet, feel superior to it. Keep them assured that they're "trying their best" or "not as bad as some people."

Fourth: If your power becomes known, even little pieces of it, like Ouija boards, spiritism, etc., make them think that it's perfectly acceptable, if possible. If not, then allow them to know that it may be "naughty" but fun and beneficial, certainly harmless. Tell them just enough to lure them into the trap. Entice them with drugs, drink and misuse of sex. Have them invoke one of your names, as in meditation. Confuse by changing the meaning of words.

Fifth: Reserve special ones to yourself who know who you are, and will worship you anyway. Fill certain psychological needs that they have. Give them powers which will keep them devoted to you. Give them plenty of thrills. Let them worship you in secret, dark places as they get further into your snare. Use fear liberally to keep them glued to you. Let your demons work quite openly through them to impress them and others, but usually disguise it as good. In the end times, you can let some of these special ones speak out openly, declaring themselves to be witches, wizards, warlocks, Satan worshippers, occult practitioners, mediums, fortune-tellers, astrologers, etc. Let others either be influenced toward them, be indifferent toward them, or think that they are "cute." Let some of these use your power to make a living or a fortune. Use TV to spread the idea that witchcraft is harmless fun.

Laugh at all of the above mentioned people — you know that they are aimed for hell and God will be grieved because of it.

Sixth: If possible, deceive even the elect. Keep them carnal as much and as long as possible to negate the will of God in their lives. Influence them to hold to the traditions of men; let them teach these as if they were doctrines of God. Blind their eyes as much as you can to all the powers of the Holy Spirit. Insist that his gifts and authority are not for them. If they recognize some gifts of the Holy Spirit, keep them suspicious of others. Make them oblivious to the fact that different members of the body of Christ are meant to have different gifts. You can convince some that all true children of God should have the same gift; you can convince others that any obvious gifts are from you. In this way you can divide and conquer. Keep all true Christians questioning the total truth of the Bible. Never leave any of them alone for very long. If they conquer natural pride, seek to fill them with spiritual pride. If they persist in worshipping God, try to deaden their minds to any thoughts of telling others of the saving power of Christ. Influence them with fear of being laughed at, or fear of offending others with the gospel. Cancel their power as witnesses for Jesus whenever you can, by whatever means.

Keep reminding them of their utter unworthiness; insist that they cannot find forgiveness yet again. Obscure the power of the blood of Jesus and its total sufficiency. Keep the laity believing that whatever needs to be done should be done by the clergy. Keep the clergyman so tied up and busy that he has little, if any, time for private prayer and study. Finally, if all your efforts against the true children of God fail, if they insist on submitting themselves to God and resisting you: Flee!

Someone has said that because of the darkness in their own souls, people choose to worship a "dark god." This is reflected all around the world as we look at the hideous idols men worship. In virtually every primitive culture, there is a horrible god; one which is evil and demands (or has demanded) human sacrifice. These dark gods are fearsome and fierce and bloodthirsty. Fearing them, people obey. This is "Baalim" — Satan. Compare our horror films and Halloween "observance." Or, as noted above, Satan sometimes disguises himself as an "angel of light" in order to influence civilized people. This "angel of light" disguise is a tremendous effective counterfeit. A professional counterfeiter would go to much time, expense, and trouble to make sure he had the best of everything. He would get the finest paper, ink, engraving, printing; everything would appear as genuine as possible. But one thing is wrong: it is not genuine.

In just the same way, Satan's most effective imitation is that which is closest to God's way, without being real: being close enough to deceive is the object.

In America, Satan's best ploy is a congregation of upright, moral, clean, attractive, kind people; people who will draw others into their group. Once there, what will they hear? Half-truths, plausible lies, a crippled Bible, an occasional mention of the name of Jesus or God; but never the truth that Jesus died as our personal substitute, or rose again to give us eternal life, or that each individual must make a personal decision for Christ in order to be a Christian. The new birth is never explained. No call is made to respond personally to the invitation of God. The gift of salvation is not discussed. The power of the blood of Jesus is never taught, nor is the indwelling Holy Spirit.

This is Satan's greatest triumph. It seems so close to the truth that millions have been fooled by it. They are lulled by it into a false sense of security, and, believing themselves already to be children of God, they are hopelessly lost. Confirmation classes are confirmed to nothing. Baptisms are performed on those who are not believers. "Busy work" replaces Bible study. Bazaars replace prayer. "Come to church" replaces "come to Jesus Christ." Devotion to denomination or congregation replaces devotion to God. The church becomes a social club; anyone can join. No one is "rude" enough to ask newcomers whether they are born again believers. Some churches even actually support occult studies, and the people see nothing wrong with it! They claim to be "searching for God."

Pathetic though it is, the above is a picture of most churches in the United States and elsewhere today. Praise God, however, there are exceptions! In some churches, the Word of God is faithfully taught. In order to join the church, the membership candidate must be able to testify to his faith in a risen, living, personal Jesus Christ. They must be born-again believers. They must testify to a willingness to obey Jesus Christ and trust him. Although members are of necessity on different levels, some more carnal, some less, the members of a congregation such as this show the love of God toward each other and in their lives. These churches are all too few, but they are there, and they are well worth seeking out.

A church such as I have just described is a delight to God; but oh, how Satan hates it!

St. Paul tells us that Satan is a master of disguise.

> Satan himself is transformed into an angel of light. Therefore, it is no great thing if his ministers also be transformed as the ministers of righteousness (2 Corinthians 11:14-15).

Don't believe whatever anyone says who happens to be a "minister" — there are all kinds. In verse 13 of the same chapter we are told of these:

> For such are false apostles, deceitful workers, transforming themselves into the apostles of Christ.

In Galatians 1:7-8, Paul says,

> There be some that trouble you, and would pervert the gospel of Christ. But though we, or an angel from heaven, preach **any other gospel** to you than that which we have preached unto you, let him be accursed.

Such false teachers may be fully aware that they are serving Satan, or they may be deceived themselves. In any case, they will have a terrible price to pay. If you doubt this, just read Ezekiel 34!

John the Beloved warns us to be very careful whom we believe. He states:

> Dearly loved friends, don't always believe everything you hear just because someone says it is a message from God: test it first to see if it really is. For there are many false teachers around, and the way to find out if their message is from the Holy Spirit is to ask: Does it really agree that Jesus Christ, God's Son, actually became man with a human body? If so, then the message is from God. If not, the message is not from God but from one who is against Christ, like the 'Antichrist' you have heard about

> who is going to come, and his attitude of enmity against Christ is already abroad in the world (1 John 4:1-3 LB).

It is their doctrine that identifies false teachers and prophets. If their doctrine is wrong, avoid them as you would a plague. They are just as deadly, even if their lives are above reproach. Remember the counterfeiter. In religious matters, any false teacher is serving Satan, whether they know it or not.

The scriptures insist that Satan is the prince of this world, even though God is the one who created it. In Genesis 1:26, God gave mankind dominion over the earth and all that was in it. But when sin entered the human race, that dominion was legally handed over to the tempter as his spoils of battle.

Hal Lindsey says,

> Jesus certainly knew Satan had won legal right to the world. When Satan personally tempted Jesus, displaying at the time his ability to deceive, the Scriptures say, 'And the devil said to Him, I will give to You all this domain and its glory; for it has been handed over to me, and I give it to whomever I wish (Luke 4:6 NAS).'[2]

J. Stafford Wright also comments on this legal right of Satan to rule the earth.

> According to Scripture, the primary aim of Satan is to organize a world system from which God is excluded. There is no reason to think he was lying when he told Jesus that all the authority and glory of the world system was his to give to anyone he wishes. But Jesus refused the gift, which would have meant power without salvation, and chose to go forward to the death on the cross that would cast out 'the ruler of this world (John 12:31-32)' who, in spite of all his efforts, could not make any claim upon the Savior (John 14:30). At the cross, Jesus disarmed Satan

and his associates by taking upon Himself the sins which gave them a hold on the human race (Colossians 2:14-15). Yet Satan still has the power to blind humans to the victory that can free them. The most trenchant verses are 2 Corinthians 4:4.

> The god of this world has blinded the minds of the unbelieving, that they might not see the light of the gospel or the glory of Christ, who is the image of God.

and 1 John 5:19,

> We know that we are of God, and the whole world lies in the power of the evil one.[3]

Jesus acknowledged the existence of the kingdom of Satan when he asked, "And if Satan cast out Satan, he is divided against himself; how then shall his kingdom stand? "(Matthew 12:26)

Jesus said, "The prince of this world cometh, and hath nothing in me." Satan has no foothold whatsoever in Jesus. In Luke 4:1-13, Jesus refused absolutely all of Satan's temptations. So Satan failed to become prince of Jesus, but he is still temporarily prince of this world.

For proof of this, all we need to do is look around. Look at the wars, hatred, envy, pride, cruelty, crime, injustice, poverty. Sinful man has done it all, tempted to it by Satan, the god of this world. The "exceeding sinfulness of sin" is revealed even more so when we realize that Satan even persuades man to put the blame for all of this on God!

From the Heavenly Father proceeds good health, love, peace, joy, beauty of all kinds. Satan has twisted everything he could and then tries to convince us that the evil comes from God! There will be no disease or tears of ugliness of any sort in heaven where God reigns. Neither can God be accused of cruelty in creating hell. It was not meant for man, ever. It was created for Satan and the angels which fell in rebellion with him (Matthew 25:41). Any humans there will be there by their own choice; having rejected God's Son, they have chosen Satan. (See Like 19:14)

The burning of incense and taking of drugs has always been associated with the worship of Satan. It's no accident that in these end times there is an upsurge in these two. Sorcery and drugs are so closely connected they even have the same Greek root word: **pharmakeia**. Witchcraft and drug use go hand-in-hand. When we consider the fate of ordinary people drawn into drug use, can there be any doubt that Satan is behind it?

Satan exploits our mistakes in every aspect of life, particularly religious error.

Dr. Merrill Unger says:

> Skepticism and ignorance concerning the Word of God produce appalling misapprehensions of reality. Men who deny the existence of Satan and demons betray their... ignorance of significant portions of the Bible.
>
> This is the plight of many liberal churchmen and of untrained Christians. They leave the safe moorings of the Word of God and are caught in the swirling currents of occult fortune telling, spiritism, magic, and false cults. A notable example is the late Bishop James A. Pike, who in September, 1967, allegedly communicated in a televised seance with his deceased son (a suicide) through a well-known medium, Arthur Ford (now deceased), who was at the same time a Disciples of Christ minister. This sensational seance startled people all over the world and alerted Bible students to the reality of modern occultism and traffic in demonism.
>
> The tragic picture today includes the well-meaning but

ill-taught Christian who professes to believe and honor the Word of God. Such a Christian, through ignorance of what the Bible teaches may naively become the victim of the fallacious reasoning that since God can heal and perform miracles, then every case of healing and everything that passes for a miracle is from God. In seeking to be healed or helped, Christians may become involved in some form of demon-energized magic.

Satan knows biblical terminology. He is also a master in masquerading under the guise of divine power. Alleged miraculous cures or manifestations often are accompanied by doctrinal errors. Every believer should recognize that Satan can use doctrinal errors to his advantage, but he cannot overcome the Christian's deference in God's Holy Word! This is our bulwark against demon incursion.

In the measure that we neglect or abandon the Word of God, demonism flourishes. Ignorance of biblical truth breeds gullibility. Deception is easy when the Word of God is not taught accurately. We are ready to believe anything when we cannot evaluate it in the light of biblical truth (1 John 4:1-6).

The contemporary Church lacks awareness of its true spiritual dimension and power. As a result many are seeking spiritual direction and help from organizations that stress psychic phenomena and experiences, such as *The Religious Research Foundation of America (RRFA), the Association for Research and Enlightenment (ARE), Inner Peace Movement (IPM), and the Spiritual Frontiers Fellowship (SFF).*

Others are turning to the delusions of spiritualism and to fortune-tellers for guidance. They neglect the Bible and seek enlightenment and comfort in the literature of occultism and metaphysics. Books such as *A Gift of Prophecy: The Phenomenal Jeane Dixon, Edgar Cayce: The Sleeping Prophet, Nothing So Strange*, and *The Search for Bridey Murphey* have enjoyed a phenomenal sale. All types of metaphysical literature are inundating the market, especially books on astrology, the ancient, pseudoscientific art cultivated by King Nebuchadnezzar (Daniel 2:2).[4]

As a type of pagan divination, astrology invites the activity of demon spirits because it originated in star worship and seeks secret knowledge in opposition to God's will and God's Word. When an Israelite became implicated in star worship, sentence of death by stoning was pronounced upon him, emphasizing the flagrant violation of the first commandment such apostasy entailed (Deuteronomy 17:1-5, Exodus 20:1-5). Since astrology originated in idolatry, it invited the interference of demonic powers of the air (Ephesians 2:2), who seek to draw men away from the adoration of the one true God.[5]

Satan's invisible servants, demons, exercise their vast powers most vividly through his visible servants: witches, wizards, sorcerers, trance channelers, astrologers, etc.

Modern witchcraft is a religion which practices magic and sorcery. Many witches are mediums; consultors of "familiar spirits (1 Samuel 28)". Some worship Satan knowingly, some worship him indirectly as the "Queen of Heaven" or "Mother Goddess" (See Jeremiah 44:15-30), or a host of other names. They often claim that their power comes from God. This is exactly what their master, the "father of lies," would have them say.

Witchcraft offers some temporary benefits to those who follow it. (1) It offers hope that it will solve their personal problems. (2) It gets them the attention as "special" which they crave. (3) It provides an opportunity to talk about and experience the supernatural. (4) It provides an excuse for drug use and sex abuse. (5) As their occult powers grow, other people may fear them and give in to their wishes. (6) It approves of doing exactly whatever you want to do. Users of both "white" and "black" magic are free to use it for selfish and harmful purposes. (7) It can open otherwise hidden knowledge. (8) It can make them rich, maybe famous.

The Bible never says that the occult does not have power. (See Exodus 7:11 and 12.) We are just warned to avoid it and even to actively destroy the occult and to win for Jesus Christ those who practice it.

> There shall not be found among you anyone who maketh his son or his daughter pass through the fire, or who useth divination, or an observer of times, or an enchanter, or a witch, or a charmer, or a consulter of mediums, or a wizard, or a necromancer. For all that do these things are an abomination unto the Lord (Deuteronomy 18:10-12).

In Leviticus 19:31, God says,

> Regard not them that have familiar spirits, neither seek after wizards, to be defiled by them: I am the Lord your God.

In Leviticus 20:6, God says,

> And the soul that turneth after such as have familiar spirits, and after wizards, to play the harlot after them, I will even set my face against that soul, and will cut him off from among his people.

> A man also or woman who hath a familiar spirit, or who is a wizard, shall surely be put to death: they shall stone

> them with stones, their blood shall be upon them [selves] (Leviticus 20:27).
>
> Therefore, hearken not to your prophets, nor to your diviners, nor to your dreamers, nor to your enchanters, nor to your sorcerers...For they prophesy a lie unto you (Jeremiah 27:9-10).

In the Old Testament, King Saul had deliberately disobeyed God's instructions. The prophet Samuel let him know how serious this really was, telling him he certainly should have obeyed: "For rebellion is as bad as the sin of witchcraft" (1 Samuel 15:23 LB). Saul lost the kingdom. In the New Testament, witchcraft is listed among the "works of the flesh." There we are told that "they who do such things shall not inherit the kingdom of God (Galatians 5:19-21)."

As I have said before, reincarnation is one of the basic tenets of witchcraft. One self-confessed witch has even written a book about it. So have deluded celebrities, with much fanfare. The spirit of witchcraft is to control other people. The ancient symbol of witchcraft is a cross upside down, broken and contained. Now renamed the "Peace Symbol" it is often displayed even in Christian churches!

People who have been in bondage to the occult world often find themselves being drawn toward it again. This is illustrated in the Bible in the life of Simon the sorcerer. He had become a true believer in Jesus and had been baptized, but the temptation to use special powers for himself had not left him. He tried to buy the power of the Holy Spirit from Peter (Acts 8:9-24).

In a documentary film on witchcraft, one young woman tells how she participated in the ritual murder of a baby. At the time it seemed to her a beautiful experience. She also told how she had been admitted to a coven: "You have to have an inheritance." She had had occult practitioners in the family, and through this, Satan had claimed her. She said, "Our mission was to destroy everyone we could, by whatever means we could." This young woman is one of the fortunate few who have found their way out of this mess to the Savior.

People involved in the occult world gradually become fearful and superstitious. Fear is Satan's objective because it keeps them tied to him. It keeps on reinforcing more and more occult involvement. They become afraid to make a move without, for instance, the horoscope or card direction. All of life's decisions for them become based on other control. This control is in the hands of Satan, who wants only to destroy them. One young witch said to a friend of mine, "Yes, I worship Satan. I use the Satan Bible. Why shouldn't I? I get everything I want. I don't need your Jesus." But the tragic end for her and others like her is described in Isaiah 47:8-15, which says, in part,
"desolation shall come upon thee suddenly...none shall save thee."

All of this was brought to life for me in a very real way when I met a young woman I'll call Claire. She had been deeply involved in Satan worship and witchcraft for several years when I met her. I was able to explain to her that God loves her in a personal way. We had a long conversation, and, by the end of it, she understood completely about the saving power of Jesus and how to get it. Claire really wanted to accept Jesus Christ as her personal Savior. But she was afraid to. She knew very well at first hand the power of Satan; she had experienced it all too often. She was terrified of what Satan would do to her if she turned to Christ. I could not convince her that God's power is greater or that she would be protected from Satan. She also felt that her sins were too great to ask for forgiveness. Her fear was real: she was afraid to get out of the trap and afraid to stay in.

Claire's fear kept her from listening to God's promise:

> Come now, and let us reason together, saith the Lord: though your sins be as scarlet, they shall be as white as snow; though they be red like crimson, they shall be as wool (Isaiah 1:18).

Claire could have found both forgiveness and protection if she had asked for it. And eternal life. She may find these things yet, through Jesus. But we never know which is our last chance for salvation. She may never again be so near.

As every good soldier knows, the best defense is a good offense. "Submit yourselves, therefore, to God. Resist the devil and he will flee from you!" Sage advice from James 4:7.

Satan, the father of lies, has great power, but hear God's promise to his children: "Behold, I give unto you power...over all the power of the enemy and nothing shall by any means hurt you. (Luke 10:19)." John, through the inspiration of the Holy Spirit says to true believers:

> Ye are of God, little children, and have overcome them, because greater is he that is in you, than he that is in the world (1 John 4:4).

God's power in us, the indwelling Holy Spirit, does have greater strength than Satan does. We need not be helpless before these evil forces.

> If we say that we have no sin, we deceive ourselves, and the truth is not in us. If we confess our sin, he is faithful and just to forgive us our sins, and to cleanse us from all unrighteousness (1 John 1:8,9).

First, we must agree with God about our sin, ask him to wash it away through the blood of Jesus and we will be cleansed. Second, repent (turn from) that sin. Third, ask Christ to come into your heart and life. Then we can "put on the whole armor of God" as described in Ephesians 6:11-18. And that armor is needed!

Wherever Satan has power, he will not give it up easily. His delusions and oppression may increase for a while. Anyone who has wandered into Satan's territory is a legal prisoner of war. Getting out can be a struggle.[6]

If anyone wishes to be free, the sooner the better. This is because Satan's grip tightens with time. Consider the criminal, the harlot, the alcoholic, any kind of addict. The longer they remain in their sin, the harder it becomes to be extricated from it. But Jesus said, "If the Son [himself] therefore shall make you free, ye shall be free indeed (John 8:36)."

Some may say,

> But you don't understand. I'm not deeply involved in this. It's like a game, and it's not dangerous. I'm not even sure I really believe it.

If thoughts like these are yours, you are hooked! Take it from a fish that got away from that very snare of Satan.

As Hal Lindsey has wisely said, "A little dabble do ya."[7] I fervently recommend his book, *Satan is Alive and Well on Planet Earth.*[8]

Lindsey tells in detail how we can bring about the defeat of Satan in our lives.[9] So does C. S. Lovett in *Dealing With The Devil*[10]; and Dr. Kurt Koch in *Occult Bondage and Deliverance.*[11]

Don't imagine you can defeat Satan on your own without Christ. You haven't got a chance. But a Christian, indwelt by the Holy Spirit and leaning on the Lord's strength will positively win the war. God's promise is, "submit yourselves therefore to God. Resist the devil and he will flee from you."

FOURTEEN

Edgar Cayce

As I mentioned earlier, books about Edgar Cayce had a profound effect on me. I had not heard of Edgar Cayce before and was astounded as I read about him in *The Sleeping Prophet*[1] and other books.[2]

Born in Kentucky in 1877, Edgar Cayce, even as a boy was markedly different. He reportedly had phantom playmates who simply disappeared if anyone else came near. He was not a good student, but found that answers came by visions, without study. His grandfather, a "water witch," could use his fingertips to cause a table to rise, or make a broom dance just by staring at it. Young Edgar's father reportedly had strange power over snakes. As is often the case, occultism persisted once established in the family.

Edgar had always been quiet and reserved as a boy, until struck on the spine by a baseball. After that, his personality began to take violent changes, alternating with normal periods. He wavered between earnest Bible study and wild friends. At twenty-four, he suddenly lost his voice and began having blinding headaches. For a year, he was unable to speak above a whisper, and had to quit a sales job to take up photography.

Doctors were unable to help him. A hypnotist tried unsuccessfully. Then someone suggested that Cayce try self-hypnosis, which he did. Although he had only a seventh-grade education, while Cayce was under the trance, he spoke like a trained physician. He accurately diagnosed the problem and prescribed treatment which restored his voice immediately.

After that he gave many medical "readings" always under trance and in virtually every case where his instructions were followed, the patient was helped, often entirely cured. Someone else had to be present to record what he said, since he was unconscious and never remembered the reading. They found that he did not even need to have the patient there; often just the name and address brought forth both description of the malady and its treatment.

Both Cayce and his wife had some misgivings about this strange ability. They knew the Bible well enough to know that the Spirit of God brings peace, not torment. They believed that he had received a gift from God, but were only too aware of the constant agony it brought. Cayce was a Sunday school teacher who voiced this suspicion:

> How do I know this came from God? I've prayed for an answer to that and there is none. There are evil forces too. This could be the devil's power in disguise using me as an innocent tool to destroy others."[3]

Every time his suspicions caused him to refuse to give "readings," he would lose his voice, until a hypnotic treatment would restore it. This frightening trilogy occurred again and again.

He began to recognize that he was losing control of his life, but for a long time still clung to the Bible as the inspired word of God. Eventually, he was called before the board of the church and questioned about his readings. He promised to stop them, but could not keep that promise.

One day he sat by a stove shivering uncontrollably when he suddenly fainted and fell to the floor. Two front teeth were broken as friends tried to get liquid down his throat. Doctors came, pronounced him dead and left. One doctor remained behind who tried hypnotic suggestion. Cayce finally revived and realized that his very life depended on continuing the psychic readings.

But to his credit, Cayce was steadfast in his refusal to cash in on his "gift" despite continuing financial troubles. Others tried cashing in on it, predictably, in every way from the wheat market to coal vein location, from gambling to crime solving. However, most of these "uses" left him exhausted, and later business ventures of his own failed despite promises in his own readings.

On October 9, 1910, the New York Times publicized Cayce's strange powers and thousands of letters asking for help descended on him. He tried to help others, even though his personal life was hounded by one disaster after another. One of their children died, Mrs. Cayce became seriously ill, poverty became bankruptcy when a mysterious fire destroyed the photography studio. Then another child was severely burned by flash powder. Fire broke out in his home, and Cayce became very depressed, then lost his voice again. He went into a trance and had a new experience which drew him into spiritualism. Because of his religious inclinations and fundamental background and knowledge of the scriptures, it took the spirits a long time to accomplish this breakthrough. After spiritualism, astrology became of interest to him, and he began to include it in readings.

Then in 1923, Cayce was contacted by Arthur Lammers, described by some as "wealthy religious adventurer." Lammers was interested in astrology and in Theosophy, a cult which teaches reincarnation and karma. Until this, Cayce's readings had been primarily on healing, but Lammers had another kind of question. He wanted Cayce to confirm his new religious ideas. Cayce agreed to answer his questions while entranced. Lammers asked age old questions such as,

> "What is the human soul? Where did it come from and where does it go? Why are we born and what becomes of us after death? Is man eternally damned or eternally blessed on the basis of his conduct?[4]

(All of these questions are answered in the Bible.)

In these readings, the spirits revealed through Cayce for the first time the teachings of reincarnation. Cayce was horrified. He knew very well that God's word teaches no such thing. Lammers insisted that Jesus taught Nicodemus reincarnation when he spoke of being born again. Cayce became confused by this twisted reasoning.

Lammers' misunderstanding, his insistence that his faulty interpretation was right, plus Cayce's accumulated worries over the years had worn him to the point that despite his knowledge, he accepted wrong as right.

One is reminded of Communist brainwashing techniques. The theory is that if you wear a man down enough, get him tired enough, insist loud and long enough, you can make him believe the grossest of lies. Lammers had plenty of help. As St. Paul says,

> For we wrestle not against flesh and blood, but against principalities, against powers, against the rulers of the

darkness of this world, against spiritual wickedness in high places (Ephesians 6:12).

How very sad that Cayce had had so strong a belief in the fundamental truths of God's word, only to be dragged away from his only chance for peace. He was afraid that "his subconscious faculties had suddenly been commandeered by the forces of evil." Once he said, "If ever the devil was going to play a trick on me, this would be it." But even in the face of this realization, he seemed helpless to do anything about it.

Once Cayce had accepted reincarnation, it was natural to tell people about their "former lives" in "life readings." This he did, many times, often citing several lives. It seems that people usually heard what would please or titillate them most. No doubt these readings drastically affected many lives. Over a period of forty-three years, Cayce gave telepathic-clairvoyant readings for more than six thousand different people. These are preserved in Virginia Beach, Virginia, at the headquarters of the "Association for Research and Enlightenment, Inc." People comb these records for meaning and build their lives around what he said, ignoring the very first commandment, "Thou shalt have no other gods before me (Exodus 20:3)."

One of the most pathetic results of Cayce's surrender to other powers was his altered position on the identity of Jesus Christ. He had always known that Jesus was the Christ, the unique and perfect Son of God. Now he began to separate Jesus from Christ, by referring to him as Jesus, who **became** the Christ.[5] Apparently his name "Immanuel," which means "God with us (Isaiah 7:14)," slipped Cayce's mind altogether, for he began to speak of other lives lived by Jesus.[6] These other people were sinners, definitely NOT "God with us." Among other Bible characters, Cayce (rather, someone using his body), claimed that Jesus had been Adam![7] Yet the Bible clearly contrasts the two:

What a contrast between Adam and Christ who was yet to come! And what a difference between man's sin and God's forgiveness! For this one man, Adam, brought death to many through his sin. But this one man, Jesus Christ, brought forgiveness to many through God's mercy. Adam's one sin brought the penalty of death to many, while Christ freely takes away many sins and gives glorious life instead. The sin of this one man, Adam, caused death to be king over all, but all who will take God's gift of forgiveness and acquittal are kings of life because of this one man, Jesus Christ. Yes, Adam's sin brought punishment to all, but Christ's righteousness makes men right with God, so that they can live. Adam caused many to be sinners because he disobeyed God, and Christ caused many to be made acceptable to God because he obeyed (Romans 5:14b-19 LB).

What slanderous blasphemy to call Adam and Christ one and the same man! No, Jesus Christ's substitutionary death for us is acceptable to God because he is, was, and always shall be perfect and sinless. "Jesus Christ, the same yesterday, and today, and forever (Hebrews 13:8)."

John, the disciple most beloved by Jesus tells us:

> But do not trust any and every spirit, my friends; test the spirits, to see whether they are from God, for among those who have gone out into the world there are many prophets falsely inspired. This is how we may recognize the Spirit of God: every spirit which acknowledges that Jesus Christ has come in the flesh is from God, and every spirit which does not thus acknowledge Jesus is not from God. This is what is meant by 'Antichrist'; you have been told that he was to come, and here he is, in the world already (1 John 4:1-3 NEB)!

How does Cayce stand this acid test? Perhaps in his waking state he did, only God knows that answer. The wheat and tares grow together in the same field. Both look like wheat.

While "sleeping," Cayce, or someone else speaking through him, denied the deity of Christ by claiming that he had sinned.[8] If Christ is God in the flesh as the Bible teaches, then he was incapable of sin, because of his perfection. Even so, he was tempted in every point, since he was also truly man. But Cayce said that Jesus had been Adam (the human introducer of sin into the world) as well as other sinful incarnations. Therefore, Cayce has proved to be a false teacher, in the spirit of antichrist. Did he agree that Jesus Christ, God's Son, actually became man with a human body? No, he did not. He claimed that Jesus required thirty lives to attain perfection.[9] That which is perfect need not work to become perfect.

In the Old Testament, a lamb was slain to cover the sins of the people. These lambs were symbolic of the Lamb to come: innocent and sinless. Only the blood of a perfect, sinless and innocent being such as a lamb could even picture the forgiveness of sin through Christ. Jesus Christ was recognized by John the Baptist: "Behold the Lamb of God! (John 1:29, 36)." 1 Peter 1:18, 19 says that we are not redeemed by vain things or traditions from our fathers: "But with the precious blood of Christ, as of a lamb without blemish and without spot."

If Jesus had been Adam, or any other sinner, the blemish would be there. Christ's sacrifice was accepted because he was perfect and spotless. "The Lamb slain from the foundation of the world (Revelations 13-8)" would not have been acceptable if he had **ever** sinned.

In an effort to answer the question, Why did Jesus have to be baptized?, Cayce invented four baptisms: earth, air, water and fire.[10] This insults God's word not only by using astrological terms, but also by denying the two true baptisms: water and Spirit.

In his book, *Edgar Cayce's Story of Jesus*, Jeffrey Furst says regarding Jesus' baptism,

> When the actual Adam was so purified (by baptism) by John the Baptist, God's voice was heard to proclaim, 'This is my first begotten Son, in whom I am well pleased.' Then to (sic), the fact that Jesus required baptism may further substantiate his role as Adam, since there, He had sinned.[11]

Wrong, wrong, wrong!

The Bible says,

> Then Jesus arrived from Galilee at the Jordan coming to John, to be baptized by him. But John tried to prevent Him, saying, 'I have need to be baptized by you, and do You come to me?' But Jesus answering said to him, 'Permit it at this time; for in this way it is fitting for us to fulfill all righteousness.' Then he permitted Him. And after being baptized, Jesus went up immediately from the water; and behold, the heavens were opened, and he saw the Spirit of God descending down as a dove, and coming upon Him, and behold, a voice out of the heavens saying, 'This is My beloved Son, in whom I am well pleased (Matthew 3:13-17 NAS).

Jesus had never sinned. He was baptized (1) as an example to us, (2) to symbolize his (and our) death, burial, and resurrection, (3) as the Father and Holy Spirit right then both publicly acknowledged the beginning of his ministry, and (4) according to Jesus' own words, it was the righteous thing to do (see also Romans 6:3-4).

> Little children, let no one deceive you: the one who practices sin is of the devil; for the devil has sinned from

the beginning. The Son of God appeared for this purpose, that he might destroy the works of the devil (1 John 3:7, 8).

In addition to being righteous, baptism is an individual and personal response to belief in Christ (trusting his work only) and receiving him as Lord and Savior. First comes true belief, then baptism. Besides an act of obedience, it is a public declaration of faith in Christ and the believer's own future resurrection. Baptism is also the symbol of death to sin and a new life (the life of the Spirit) indwelling the believer. Thus, the baptism of Jesus provides us with a clear and beautiful illustration of the baptism of the Holy Spirit.

Before I go on, I must return for a moment to Furst's momentous slip. He quotes God as saying, "This is my **first begotten** Son." Whether it is Furst's or Cayce's mistake is unclear; in any case, it is incorrect. The witnesses heard God's voice saying, "This is my **beloved** Son, in whom I am well pleased (Matthew 3:17)."[12]

Over and over again, the Bible tells us that Jesus is the ONLY begotten Son (John 3:16 and John 1:18, for examples). Others, however, may become joint heirs with Christ, if they accept God's way to himself. There is only one Christ; though we may become **like** him, we will never become truly Messiah. Jesus said, "**I** am the way, the truth, and the life; no man cometh unto the Father, but by me (John 14:6)." There's a big difference between a doctor, for instance, and "like a doctor."

Some translations of the Bible are "like a Bible" in this way. John 1:1 refers to Jesus as the Word — God's communication to mankind. "In the beginning was the Word, and the Word was with God, and the Word was God." This is the true rendering from the Greek — yet some "like-a-Bibles" say, "the Word was a god." Such a simple change to make the truth a lie!

Here's an illustration of what I mean. Suppose that 200 years ago, an ancestor of yours kept a meticulous diary which revealed him as the fine and upright man he surely was. After his death, a bitter foe got possession of that diary; and to cover his changes, he simply made a copy, changing a few words here and there. The result? Whatever the rewriter wanted! Family tradition knew the existence of the diary, confirmed some parts as true; and since the original had disappeared, your ancestor is believed by one and all to be a black-hearted scoundrel!

To take the analogy a little further, suppose my son got a letter which looked like my writing, bore my signature, seemed authentic in every way, but urged him to commit a crime. Because he knows me and my characteristics, he would not be fooled. Pending changes in certain editions of the Bible are being planned by groups who choose to deliberately obscure and malign God's character with falsehood. Some of these are backed by church groups which have been thoroughly infiltrated by unbelievers. Don't be fooled by false "Bibles!" They will be called Bibles but will be counterfeit.

What the original says matters plenty! One cult makes frequent changes in their "like-a-Bible" to suit their current fancy, all the while claiming to be God's friends. All pseudo-Christian groups I know of supplement the Bible with founder's writings which contradict the Spirit-inspired Word of God. Or, they mangle the words which are there and claim that what's left may or may not be so, depending on your point of view! For reasons already detailed in Chapter 10, we know today's Bible is reliable.

Without trust in God's word, finding the true Jesus is virtually impossible. The Jesus Christ of the Bible is true. Many people have imagined and set up their own idolized version of Jesus and worship that. In much the same way, multitudes have imagined the perfect Father as loving, but not righteous; merciful, but not just; forgiving everyone instead of being fair. It **does** matter what you believe. The Bible is the criterion.

FIFTEEN
More Cayce

> If a prophet arises among you, or a dreamer of dreams, and gives you a sign or a wonder, and the sign or wonder which he tells you comes to pass, and if he says, 'Let us go after other gods, which you have not known, and let us serve them,' you shall not listen to the words of that prophet or to that dreamer of dreams; for the Lord your God is testing you, to know whether you love the Lord your God with all your heart and with all your soul. You shall walk after the Lord your God and fear him, and keep his commandments and obey his voice, and you shall serve him and cleave to him (Deuteronomy 13:1-4 RSV).

How does Edgar Cayce measure up here? Did he advise anyone to follow after other gods?

On page 48 of the book, *Edgar Cayce's Story of Jesus*, by Jeffrey Furst, the author says:

> With these headings we have broached the subject of Planetary influences and astrology in relationship to soul

> development. It is significant that of the 2,500 Life Readings in the Cayce files, almost all refer to past lives or incarnations with specific astrological or planetary influences bearing on the present.[1]

He's right. This is very significant indeed since the Bible specifically warns against "observers of times," meaning astrologers.

> There shall not be found among you anyone who maketh his son or his daughter pass through the fire, or who useth divination, or an observer of times, or an enchanter, or a witch, or a charmer, or a consulter of mediums, or a wizard, or a necromancer. For all that do these things are an abomination unto the Lord (Deuteronomy 18:10-12).

The Chaldeans and the Babylonians lived in the area of the Persian Gulf, and both civilizations practiced astrology, which was a part of "mystery religions."

> The astrological lore of the region was so famous that the very names Chaldean and Babylonian came to mean astrology.[2]

The name "Babylonian" as used in the Bible refers often to false religions. The Book of Revelation, Chapter 18, tells how Babylon, false religion, will finally fall. Ancient Babylon's main religion was "mystery" teaching. Today we see a great upsurge in that religion. In America, this is due largely to the influence of Edgar Cayce.

Those who love the Lord their God with all their heart and soul do not put other gods before him. And yet we find thousands of people obsessed, not with God, but with concern about what the stars mean to them. Whatever a person holds first in their life and thoughts and heart and soul, that is their religion. Sometimes it's God: most often it's false gods of nature or self. Often it's a god of their own imaginings rather than the revealed God of the Bible. Many people today instead of keeping their eyes fixed on God, are hungrily reading and memorizing, for instance, what Edgar Cayce, an astrologist, or a demon posing as a "wise person" has said.

But listen to what the true prophet, Isaiah, says to "Babylon," and to "the daughter of the Chaldeans:"

> You felt sure of yourself in your evil; you thought that no one could see you. Your wisdom and knowledge led you astray, and you said to yourself, 'I am God —there is no one else like me.' Disaster will come upon you and none of your magic can stop it. Ruin will come on you suddenly — ruin you never dreamed of! Keep all your magic spells and charms; you have used them since you were young. Perhaps they will be of some help to you; perhaps you can frighten your enemies. You are powerless in spite of the advice you get. Let your astrologers come forward and save you — those people who study the stars, who map out the zones of the heavens and tell you from month to month what is going to happen to you. They will be like bits of straw, and a fire will burn them up! They will not even be able to save themselves — the flames will be too hot for them, not a cozy fire to warm themselves by. That is all the good they will do you — those astrologers you've consulted all your life. They all will leave you and go their own way, and none will be left to save you (Isaiah 47:10-15 TEV).

Edgar Cayce kept referring to astrology, even though the astrologists clearly can't save either themselves or others from the power of the flame to come. His teachings have turned some people's thoughts from the Living God toward their own "life readings." No doubt this causes over-emphasis on self. Satan told Eve, "Ye shall be as gods." We are to turn to God for guidance. Trying to find "secret knowledge" not revealed in God's word is always ultimately disastrous.

An unknown person using Cayce's body and a different voice suggested worship of other gods. Furst says the voice claimed to be John (apparently John the Beloved); once it said it was actor John Drew. This kind of mediumistic claim is boringly common. (Mediums, incidentally, are damned throughout the Bible.) Sometimes the strange voice using Cayce's body claimed to be an "angel," Halaliel. Then one who identified himself as "Michael, Lord of the Way."[3] In each of several instances, this "person" ordered those present to bow their heads. There is no place in scripture where an angel ever asked for reverence for himself. In fact, in Revelation 19:10, John the Beloved, having been spoken to by an angel, says,

> Then I fell down at his feet to worship him, but he said, 'No! Don't! For I am a servant of God just as you are, and as your brother Christians are, who testify of their faith in Jesus. The purpose of all prophecy and of all I have shown you is to tell about Jesus' (Revelation 19:10 LB).

But this "angel" speaking through Cayce not only demanded reverence, he had the brass to call himself "Lord." He also gave vague messages rather than specific directions. Check through your Bible for the behavior patterns of genuine angels. They never ask for worship: they always glorify God instead of self; they always had a definite message, usually with an urgency such as "Make haste." They never referred to themselves as Lord of anything; although, significantly, that is precisely what Satan has always wanted — to be worshipped as God.

Therefore, this demand for reverence is a dead giveaway of its Satanic origin.

If Cayce was a born-again Christian, could he possibly have still been used of Satan to delude people? Yes, because he did not overcome the spirits which oppressed him. The Bible leaves no doubt that God's power is greater than Satan's, but God's power must be called upon in order to be used. The darkened lamp has electricity available, but light is there only when the switch is turned on. Missionaries and other leaders all around the world often tell of true Christians who are influenced or even actually possessed of dark spirits. (see Chapter 12)

The Cayce healings seemed genuine. However, not all healings need come from God. Pagans worshipping idols are sometimes truly healed, frequently only under the condition that they remain loyal in worshipping the idol, just like Cayce himself. He finally realized that his voice and even his life depended on his willingness to give readings. If Cayce was truly unsaved, God's power was not available to him at all and Satan would have no restraint.

The vast interest in America today in reincarnation and its attendant errors is traceable in large part to Edgar Cayce. He opened himself to "powers of the air," and Satan's will is being done because of it. Multitudes are being deluded by these false teachings and turned from the truth of the scripture because of them.

Jesus Christ personally gives this warning:

> For there shall arise false Christs, and false prophets, and shall show great signs and wonders, insomuch that, if it were possible, they shall deceive the very elect (Matthew 24:24).

Jesus also cautions us:

> Beware of false prophets, who come to you in sheep's

> clothing, but inwardly they are ravening wolves. Ye shall know them by their fruits (Matthew 7:15, 16).

It should go without saying that a true prophet of God would turn people away from false beliefs. By the same token, a false prophet would turn people away from the truth. Sorry to say, this is what Edgar Cayce allowed himself to do. He showed great signs, and great wonders, and as the Lord has said, we shall know him by his fruits.

What are the fruits of the teachings of Edgar Cayce? (1) A hunger for "secret" knowledge. (2) A faulty interpretation of, or a turning away from, the Holy Word of God. (3) An upsurge in acceptance of reincarnation, which teaches salvation through works instead of grace. (4) A renewal of interest in astrology, repeatedly condemned in the Bible. (5) A substitution of the false gods of self, "former selves," Cayce, an imaginary Jesus or other forms of idolatry, etc. These bitter fruits will send multitudes to hell. A good comparison of Cayce vs. Christianity is given in *Understanding the Occult.*[4]

Some other teachings out of Cayce's mouth really need to be discussed. To choose just a few, let's begin with a quote from Furst's book:

> According to the (Cayce) readings, John the Beloved received his visions in deep meditation. Much of what he recorded is described as a symbolic interpretation of the mysteries as they relate to spiritual development of the human body — this in relation to the seven psychic centers, or spiritual centers, associated with the body's endocrine glands.
>
> The message of the Revelation is that each of us, through a proper approach to the body-mind-spirit principle of the body, as the Temple of the Living God, can attain to Christhood even as He did.[5]

Imagine that! In the first paragraph of the above quote, he actually says that Revelation deals with spiritual development of our endocrine glands! There is no spiritual development of the human body. Flesh is flesh and spirit is spirit. And only Christ is Christ!

Contrasting the erroneous statements quoted above, the Scofield Bible, edited by C. I. Scofield, D.D., and nine theological scholars serving on the editorial committee prefaces the Book of Revelation as follows, in part:

> The Revelation, the concluding book of the Scriptures, unfolds the great events bringing history to consummation, including the revelation of Jesus Christ at His second advent. The word 'revelation' used as the title of the book, is from the late Latin **revelatio**, which means (as does the Greek **apokalupsis**, from which the English word 'apocalypse' is derived) **disclosure of that which was previously hidden or unknown.**
>
> In the unfolding of this central theme, Jesus Christ is revealed in glory in contrast with His presentation, in the four Gospels, in His humiliation. In The Revelation Christ is seen in relationship to time as He 'who was, and who is to come' (1:4). He is related to the Church (1:9-3:22), the tribulation (4:1-19; 21), the millennial kingdom (20:1-10), and the eternal state (20:11-22; 21).
>
> Christ is presented in the book as the Ruler of the kings of the earth (1:5), the Bridegroom and Head of the Church (2:1-3:22; 19:7-9), the Lion of the tribe of Judah (5:5), the Lamb that was slain (5:6, 12, etc.), the High Priest (8:3-6), and the King and Judge (19:11-20:15).
>
> The book is a record of what the Apostle John saw and heard. Constant use is made of symbols. References to Old

> Testament events and prophecies abound. Frequent shifts of locale from earth to heaven and back to earth may be observed. It is an account of divine judgment and conflict which sweeps the whole world.
>
> Three major divisions of The Revelation must be recognized. John was commanded in 1:19 to write concerning (1) things past, 'the things which thou hast seen,' i.e., the Patmos vision (1:1-20); (2) things present, 'the things which are,' i.e., the existing churches (2:1-3:22); and (3) things future, 'the things which shall be hereafter (lit. after these),' i.e., events after the Church Age ends (4:1-22:5). It is important to observe that, beginning in Chapter 4, the book presents future events.[6]

To reduce this majestic mountain to a mythical molehill of "seven spiritual centers of the human endocrine glands" is nothing short of ludicrous.

An even more grievous error is recorded in Cayce reading 1472: "each and every soul must become, must be, the savior of some (other) soul." Jeffrey Furst says, in *The Return of Frances Willard*, page 152,

> For as the Cayce readings spell it out, no man enters the kingdom of heaven except on the arm of someone he has aided in finding that same doorway in the past.[7]

This is perhaps the most monstrous lie of all. Jesus understood his mission well. If we could save ourselves or others, he would not have needed to suffer, or indeed to have been born at all. If we could save each other, how could he claim to be the Savior of the world? Jesus said, "I am the way, the truth and the life; no man cometh to the Father, but by me." Souls are saved because **God** has opened the hearts of men to Christ. As Paul put it, "I have planted, Apollos watered, but God gave the increase."

Cayce is quoted in *Story of Jesus* as saying that Christ was created (2072-4).[8] But the Bible says that in the beginning, he already was, and that nothing was created without him (John 1).

1 Peter 1:20 says that he was foreordained before the foundation of the world. Colossians 1:16 — "All things were created by him and for him, and he is before all things, and by him all things consist." Did Cayce mean to say that Christ created himself?

A minor error, but still an error — Cayce claims Zacharias, father of John the Baptist, was slain even with his hands on the horns of the altar (5749-8).[9] This was not Zacharias, but Zechariah, written of in 2 Chronicles 24:21; this event was not during the time of Christ, but in the fifth century before. A true prophet speaking for God is incapable of error.

Sheer fantasy here — Cayce said that Mary was one of twelve young girls separated and trained by the Essenes to be available as a potential mother to the Messiah. Joseph was a member of this sect, too, according to Cayce.[10] If this were true, isn't it strange that Joseph at first determined to put her away quietly rather than marry her? (Matthew 1:19)

I know how easy it is to believe Cayce. For five years, I believed him myself. I have come to understand that the Lord allowed me to accept these false teachings so that he could show me the truth and eventually lead in the writing of this book. How this book itself came to be is an interesting story, but at this point I think it is more important to tell you why I believed Cayce.

First, I was not born again of the Spirit. This is the most important reason I fell into error. I did not know the difference between a false Christian and a real one. How could anyone recognize what is false if they don't know what the truth is? Could you identify counterfeit money from Bulgaria or Indonesia? First, you would have to be familiar with the genuine, obviously. For more than thirty years, I believed myself to be a Christian, but I was not. The indwelling Holy Spirit is what makes the difference. Ignorance of this fact is nothing to be ashamed of, since many who give their whole lives in what they believe to be the Lord's service are as lost as heathen who have never heard the name.

The one Bible passage which puzzled me more than any other was Matthew 7:21-23. Jesus says,

> Not every one that saith unto me, Lord, Lord, shall enter into the kingdom of heaven, but he that doeth the will of my Father, which is in heaven. Many will say to me in that day, Lord, Lord, have we not prophesied in thy name? and in thy name have cast out devils? and in thy name done many wonderful works? And then will I profess unto them, I never knew you: depart from me, ye that work iniquity.

They call him Lord and do great works in his name, yet they will be unacceptable!

Second, I did not have the power of discernment of the Holy Spirit within, and so had no protection whatsoever from Satan's clever deceptions. As far as I could tell, Edgar Cayce was a Christian, and **he** believed in reincarnation. He had even been a Sunday school teacher for many years. He used the name of Jesus, his words had a Biblical tone and there were reasons why I **wanted** to believe him.

Foremost among these was pride. How delicious it feels to have knowledge, real or imagined, which makes one clearly superior to the masses. I fancied that the Bible was just incomplete, and Cayce had been chosen to reveal new things. I was one of the few who knew the way things really were! This desire for secret information has landed countless millions in hell. The Bible IS complete. Everything we need to know is there.

> For I testify unto every man that heareth the words of the prophecy of this book. If any man shall add unto these things, God shall add unto him the plagues that are written in this book: And if any man shall take away from the words of the book of this prophecy, God shall take away his part out of the book of life, and out of the holy city, and from the things which are written in this book (Revelation 22:18,19).

The original sin was not an apple, but pride. Satan wished to be worshipped as God. I have heard it said that all sin traced far enough, goes back to pride. Our pride keeps us from admitting that we need a savior. Our pride makes us want to **receive** honor instead of giving it to God, who alone is worthy of praise. You've heard the old adage, "the way to hell is paved with good intentions," but it should be "the highway to hell is pride."

The born-again Christian knows beyond all shadow of doubt that he or she is going to heaven when death comes. You would think that this would make them puffed up with pride and a sense of vast superiority. Paradoxically, the exact opposite happens. When we are indwelt by the Holy Spirit, we are more aware than ever of our own unworthiness. We still sin and are more and more aware of God's mercy and grace to us. Where is room for pride here? No; rather than pride the Holy Spirit endues us with a deep concern for the souls of others, that they might share our joy and peace and future, being a new creature in Christ.

Time after time, we find Cayce using Biblical names and weaving fanciful stories around them — stories with no foundation except his word for it. It is amazing how many Bible characters Cayce seemed to find reincarnated in his day and nation! Atlantis was another favorite "former home," impossible to check. Cayce devotees keep studying his words, but the truth is that much of what he said was double-talk couched in high-flown phrases with a biblical flavor to lend what seems to be authenticity.

> But the Holy Spirit tells us clearly that in the last times some in the church will turn away from Christ and become eager followers of teachers with devil-inspired ideas. These teachers will tell lies with straight faces and do it so often that their consciences won't even bother them (1 Timothy 4:1 and 2, LB).

Just as this foretells, Edgar Cayce has led many away from the true Christ to a made-up one.

> Do bear with me and let me say what is on my heart. I am anxious for you with the deep concern of God himself — anxious that your love should be for Christ alone, just as a pure maiden saves her love for one man only, for the one who will be her husband. But I am frightened, fearing that in some way you will be led away from your pure and simple devotion to our Lord, just as Eve was deceived by Satan in the Garden of Eden. You seem so gullible; you believe whatever anyone tells you even if he is preaching **another Jesus** than the one we preach, or a different spirit than the Holy Spirit you received, or shows you a different way to be saved. You swallow it all (2 Corinthians 11:1-4 LB).

How well Paul's prophetic words fit us today!

Many other Bible prophecies predicted for the end times are also taking place right now. These include the return of Jews to Israel, their possession of Jerusalem, the rise of Russia as a world power, and so forth.

True prophecy **always** agrees with the Bible. Cayce often contradicted it.

How else can you tell true prophecy from false? What is the criteria? Listen.

> If you wonder, 'How shall we know whether the prophecy is from the Lord or not?' this is the way to know: If the thing he prophesies doesn't happen, it is not the Lord who has given him the message; he has made it up himself (Deuteronomy 18:21, 22 LB).

Cayce prophesied that Hitler would be a good force, that Atlantis would rise out of the sea around 1975, and that mainland China would be a democratic Christian country by 1968. Only false prophets give false prophecies.[11] Other failed Cayce prophecies are listed in *Dark Secrets of the New Age.*[12]

Years before his death, Edgar Cayce realized that his freedom of will had been lost.

Joseph Milliard writes:

> He felt sick and hopeless and more than a little frightened. There was no longer any use in trying to pretend he was a normal human being with a will and freedom of choice. He was not a person at all. He was a puppet controlled by forces beyond human comprehension. When unseen fingers twitched at the strings, he must dance whether he wanted to or not.[13]

In quoting the above passage, Gordon Lindsay adds:

> Can any person familiar with the Word of God conceive that such a power came from the Holy Spirit? The Holy Spirit is gentle, even as a dove; He leads and does not drive, nor make a slave out of a person. Poor Edgar Cayce was driven by a force that made his life a nightmare.[14]

Thousands of people have been deceived by a lying demon using Edgar Cayce as a medium. Of these, the most tragic was Edgar Cayce himself.

SIXTEEN

Human Reasoning — Ruth Montgomery

My early efforts to test reincarnationist theories were made difficult by the fact that most references on the subject were and still are pro-reincarnation. This makes it extremely difficult for a genuine searcher to explore both sides of the question, particularly if they find the Bible hard to understand.

Early writings of Jeanne Dixon expressed disbelief in reincarnation, but more recent writings and activities show her continual slide into the occult.[1,2] This has followed exactly the same pattern Edgar Cayce was caught in, as described in the last chapter here.

Books on reincarnation are now much more plentiful. A popular spokeswoman for this view is Ruth Montgomery, whose work deserves comment.

The following passages have brought home to me afresh the tremendous value of God's word. Human reasoning can sound so **right**, but without the authority and truth of God behind it, it's deadly. This is especially true when the words have a religious veneer, and when their author sincerely believes the errors.

On the next few pages are a number of direct quotes taken from Ruth Montgomery's book, *Here and Hereafter.*[3] My comments follow hers.

> How many hundreds of times we have recited the Lord's Prayer by rote, without pausing to grasp the awesome meaning of the line, 'Forgive us our trespasses as we forgive those who trespass against us.' Let us ponder the significance of the word 'as.' What we are actually asking God to do is to forgive us to the same degree that we forgive others. This places the burden on our own hearts. If we would have God forgive our evil thoughts and deeds, so that we can come under the law of Grace instead of the law of karma, then we must just as wholeheartedly forgive our own debtors.

Ruth Montgomery is right regarding the awesomeness of the word "as" in the Lord's Prayer. If we are unforgiving ourselves, praying to be forgiven to the same degree is dangerous business. But she goes on to say, "so that we can come under the law of Grace instead of the law of karma." A definition of grace is called for here. An acrostic can be made from the letters G R A C E, to give a good definition. "God's Riches at Christ's Expense." God's **riches**: forgiveness, heaven, eternal life, peace, joy and a sense of the love of God — at Christ's expense. The expense of the scourge, Gethsemane, the mocking, the plucking of his beard, the crown of thorns, the nailing of his hands, the piercing of his side, the wrath of God, and hell itself.[4]

Grace is always to be contrasted to law. "For whosoever shall keep the whole law, and yet offend in one point, he is guilty of all (James 2:10)." If we are under grace, we are freed from the law, which requires perfection, as Paul explains in Romans, chapters 5 and 6. The concordance in the New Scofield Reference Bible lists twenty-nine references to grace. This list is incomplete. But karma is not in the Bible once. Karma does not appear in scripture because it does not exist. Can we seriously believe that such an important doctrine would be unknown to God? I refer you to Christ himself. Though speaking on another subject, he clearly showed his attitude toward the apostles when he said, "If it were not so, I would have told you."

Every teaching of the Bible which is important for us to understand is mentioned more than once, couched in different terminology, so that it can't be misunderstood. In this way the Lord has provided cross-references, so that if we find a teaching "twistable" in one place, it will be unmistakable in another. The Bible is silent on karma because man has dreamed it up; to call it a law is heresy of the first order.

If the so-called "law of karma" did exist, it follows that God would forgive nothing, since those deeds would have to be "worked out." Yet, the entire Bible is based from cover to cover on the gracious forgiveness of God, dependent on confession and repentance.

> To love, to forgive. Is this really so hard to do, if we remember that God also created our rival, and that he loves him as compassionately as He does us? God has already forgiven both of us. Can we not do likewise?

Here again we find truth and fiction mixed. God has created both people involved and does love both. Correct. Then Ruth Montgomery says, "God has already forgiven both of us." Is that so? It is true that he loves the sinner; but he hates the sin (Zechariah 8:17). Forgiveness is not automatic. It requires repentance and confession. First John 1:9 is called "the Christian's cake of soap" for good reason — it says,

> If we confess our sins he is faithful and just to forgive us our sins, and to cleanse us from all unrighteousness.

Notice the first word — **IF**.

Yes, we should forgive others. Jesus said, "Seventy times seven (Matthew 18:22)."

> God punishes no man. We punish ourselves through the allergies, the hatreds which make us ill, and the karmic retribution that we have chosen to work out. We brought with us into this life the permanent record of our own foibles and misdeeds. Many of us carefully selected our parents, and assigned ourselves the circumstances into which we were born. If the role is a humble one, we chose it in the belief that we could best atone for past errors by enduring hardships and surmounting difficult barriers. We felt that suffering was essential to the cleansing process. Therefore, it is not "who" we are in this brief lifetime, but "what" we think and do, and how cheerfully and lovingly we meet the challenges, that matters.

Here we find the stupefying statement, "God punishes no man." There are myriads of references in God's word to hell, hades, sheol, torment and damnation. There are also twenty-nine New Testament references to hell and punishment; twenty-two came directly from the lips of Jesus. The Old Testament alone has so many references to punishment which God meted out to individuals, cities and nations, that just to name them all would take a chapter. The history of Israel would be a prime example.

God's punishment, however, is reserved for those who reject his salvation. Chastening is entirely different. Punishment connotes a vengeance; but chastening means discipline and its purpose is teaching. "For whom the Lord loveth he chasteneth (Hebrews 12:6)." Discipline and training may be difficult for his children to bear, but he loves us enough to see that we learn needed lessons. 1 Thessalonians 5:18 provides both a mountain of courage and a willingness to learn.

We do punish ourselves, that is true. Guilt, hatred, bitterness, envy, greed, etc., take a terrific toll of our bodies. Not because we have chosen it, but because we are going against the law he has written in our hearts. We were created for this reason — to glorify God (Isaiah 43:7). It is when we fail to fulfill this purpose that we suffer inwardly, and often outwardly as well.

Then there is that phrase, "work out." Ruth Montgomery says "work out." God says, "Not by works of righteousness which we have done, but according to his mercy he saved us (Titus 3:5)." "God will by **no** means clear the guilty (Exodus 34:7)." The Pharisees "trusted in themselves that they were righteous (Luke 18:9)." God says, "There is none righteous, no, not one (Roman 3:10)," and "We are all as an unclean thing, and all our righteousnesses are as filthy rags (Isaiah 64:6)." No one can cleanse but God. Jesus said, "I am the way (John 14:6)." Observe that he did not say, "You and I together are the way" —he did not say, "I am **a** way." He is the **only** way, and said so.

Our works count for nothing, except in the case of works done by a born-again Christian for the purpose of glorifying God. These works will be rewarded. "Lay up for yourselves treasures in heaven (Matthew 6:20)."

> Why do most of us fail to remember our previous lives? Because the burden of such knowledge might be more than we could comfortably bear, and because a conscious awareness of old grievances, or former skills, could interfere with the new path that we have set out upon. Just as 'the child is father of the man,' so we are the sum total of all our attitudes, conduct and experiences in ages past.

More importantly, we are busily creating the kind of person that we will become in the next lifetime, and the next.

The question, "Why do most of us fail to remember our previous lives?" has a simple truthful answer — because we had none. In Chapter Eight we explored biblical answers to the question, Do we have another chance after death? Ruth Montgomery says,

> If every man could accept the promise that he has no one except himself to blame for his misfortunes, and would resolve to atone for the error of his ways, the world could change dramatically. Warfare would disappear, for what person would dare to pursue the path of the aggressor? Who would rob, or kill, or rape if he were convinced that he was preparing a similar fate for himself? Race, sex, and religious prejudices would vanish if man knew that he himself had previously been, or in the future, would become, a Negro, an Oriental, a Catholic, a Jew, a Moslem, a Hindu, or a white woman. Rebellious youth could scarcely resent their parents if they thought that they had selected them in order to fulfill a particular mission for which they chose to be reborn: and parents might better understand their willful youngsters knowing that they may previously have been their own father, sister or formidable rival who wanted to be born to them to work out a karmic situation.

What we do now definitely does control our future after death. Jesus said, "Lay up for yourselves treasures in heaven, where neither moth nor rust doth corrupt." The greatest glory of heaven is this — we shall see him face to face. Revelation 21:2-4 speaks of the beauty of this:

> God himself shall be with them, and be their God. And God shall wipe away all tears from their eyes; and there shall be no more death, neither sorrow, nor crying, neither shall there be any more pain: for the former things are passed away.

Those who will not have him for their God will be in hell.

Ruth Montgomery paints a lovely portrait of the world as it could be if only everyone believed in reincarnation and karma. It sounds nice, but the world is destined for sin and tribulation until the final day when Christ himself will rule. Any hope not placed in him is a false hope; be it karma, good works, church membership, world peace, or reincarnation.

Again, an inconsistency in "rebellious youths — (and others) born to them to work out a karmic situation." If this were their purpose, they would not rebel. Rather, they would get on with it (but just how they are to know this is unclear).

> It is not overly important whether we believe in reincarnation. If the laws of karma and Grace are real, they will survive without our attestation. What does matter is that we conduct ourselves in such a manner that we incur no bad karmic indebtedness. The skeptic may ask, 'What if there's no such thing as karma, or reincarnation, or eternal life?' Yes, but what if there is?

As mentioned earlier, the law of grace is as real as this page and is found many times in the Bible but the "law of karma" is sheer fabrication and no reference to it can be found in the Bible.

Christ is trustworthy. We have his word and can depend on it, that mercy is gained through him alone. We must conduct ourselves in order to please God, not in fear of karmic retribution. "But without faith it is impossible to please him (Hebrews 11:6)."

The skeptic may very well ask whether karma, reincarnation and eternal life exist. We have the word of God Almighty that eternal life does indeed exist. John, the disciple perhaps closest of all to Christ, says this:

> And what is it that God has said? That he has given us eternal life, and that this life is in his Son. So whoever has God's Son has life; whoever does not have his Son, does not have life (1 John 5:11,12 LB).

Reincarnation and karma are representative of the thinking of men, not God. "Claiming themselves to be wise without God, they became utter fools instead" (Romans 1:22 LB). "The way of a fool is right in his own eyes, but he that hearkeneth unto counsel is wise" (Proverbs 12:15). "The fool rageth, and is confident" (Proverbs 14:16).

"Hath not God made foolish the wisdom of this world?" (1 Corinthians 1:20)

Indirect repayment through karma may sound right to us, but God says he will repay face-to-face:

> Know, therefore, that the Lord thy God, he is God, the faithful God, who keepeth covenant and mercy with them who love him and keep his commandments to a thousand generations, and **repayeth them who hate him to their face, to destroy them; he will not be slack to him who hateth him; he will repay him to his face** (Deuteronomy 7:9 and 10).

Man says, "I think this" or "I think that," but God says, "Thus saith the Lord."

SEVENTEEN

More Human Reasoning — Head and Cranston

In the book, *Reincarnation, An East-West Anthology*[1], Joseph Head and S. L. Cranston have listed references from (among others) both Jewish and Christian sources. These, imply the authors, are proofs of reincarnation.

These authors ignore context.

What is the most absurd thing you can imagine? Let's say that the instant you go to sleep, your most cherished possession becomes a pumpkin. The instant before you awake, it becomes normal. So you never see it as a pumpkin. That's pretty ridiculous, isn't it? But, I promise you, you could find Bible verses which would seem to say that, provided you will take those verses out of context and twist their meaning to disagree with the rest of the Bible. (Try it with "old things" in 2 Corinthians 5:17.) In this way, it is possible to come up with all kinds of weird ideas and Biblical "support" for them.

Nowhere does the inspired Word of God teach reincarnation. The proof of the Bible is in the Bible — it is a unit which proves itself. An idea taken from one place must agree with the rest of scripture, or you can be sure it has been taken out of context.

A quote from Head and Cranston's list supposedly "proving" reincarnation, from the "Judaism" section.

> [Moses addressing the Lord concerning the death of human beings] 'Thou turnest man to destruction; and sayest, Return, ye children of men. For a thousand years in thy sight are but as yesterday when it is past, and as a watch in the night (Psalm 90:3-4).'[2]

This does not teach reincarnation. Even though God must destroy men who turn from him, still he urges **their children** to repent and turn to him. Repent means, literally, "to turn from." This psalm may very well have been written just after God had sentenced the nation of Israel to wander forty years in the wilderness. None of these rebels were to be allowed to enter the promised land, but if their children would repent and turn to the Lord, **they** would be allowed to enter. Forty years to God would be less than a watch in the night. "Return" in Psalm 90 urges spiritual return to the Lord. He was willing to wait for a thousand years, if necessary.

The next verse quoted by Head and Cranston (also from the section "Judaism") is Proverbs 8:22-31. Here is a classic case of taking something out of context. The authors attribute this section to King Solomon,[3] and it is true that he was the human "pen" used by the author, the Holy Spirit. But the whole chapter, as the chapters both before and after this one, speak of wisdom. **Wisdom** is the speaker in all of Proverbs Eight. This is most positively **not** Solomon telling of his preexistence. Read the chapter for yourself. Then ask this question — in the rest of the word of God, who is the personification of wisdom? None other than Jesus Christ, the Son of God. He alone could say, as in Proverbs 8:35, "For who so findeth **me** findeth life, and shall obtain favor of the Lord." That this personification of Wisdom is the Lord Jesus Christ is borne out in the New Testament.

> Christ [is] the power of God, and the wisdom of God...Christ Jesus, who of God is made unto us wisdom, and righteousness, and sanctification, and redemption...(1 Corinthians 1:24,30).

To show biblical "support" for reincarnation, Head and Cranston next list Jeremiah 1:4, 5:[4]

> Then the word of the Lord came unto me saying, before I formed thee in the belly I knew thee; and before thou comest forth out of the womb I sanctified thee, and I ordained thee a prophet unto the nations.

It is astounding that this could be mistaken for a proof of reincarnation. The entire Bible teaches that God is all-knowing. Of **course**, he knew Jeremiah before he was born! Past, present and future are all alike to God. There is NO limit to his knowledge.

Head and Cranston further quote Ecclesiastes 1:9-11:[5]

> The thing that hath been, it is that which shall be...and there is no new thing under the sun. Is there any thing whereof it may be said, See, this is new? It hath been already of old time, which was before us. There is no remembrance of former things.

The whole context here is speaking of material **things**: that word **things** is repeated over and over again. This does not talk of people, but of the endless cycles of the material things which mankind loves. Archaeology keeps bearing this out. The human race has forgotten the water systems, plumbing, air conditioning methods and many other material comforts that men of old also enjoyed. We may think that our civilization has much that is new, but it is not necessarily so. The remembrance of these things has passed away.

Head and Cranston follow these four "proofs" from the Old Testament with several pages of quotes from Jewish writers outside the scripture. Their "evidence" is inadmissible, since it does not come from God's word. Men are free to say anything at all. But the authors do admit, "In the Old Testament itself, very little can be pointed to directly inferring rebirth (p. 83)."[6]

Then Head and Cranston begin a chapter entitled "Christianity," purporting to Biblically prove reincarnation. This chapter starts by saying,

> The ancient Jews were continually expecting the reincarnation of their great prophets. Moses was in their opinion Abel, the son of Adam, and their Messiah was to be the reincarnation of Adam himself, who had already come a second time as David.[7]

Talk about inadmissible evidence! These are opinions, not facts. The Bible does not say these things. As we have already seen, Jesus knew that some Jews held to wrong beliefs, and asked his disciples who the Jews said that he was. Their opinions were wrong. Simon Peter's statement of faith was right.

In Chapter Fourteen of this book, there are given Biblical proofs that Jesus and Adam were positively not the same man. For the same reasons, Jesus and David were not the same man. David was a sinner — read his life and see. Jesus never sinned —read his life and see. This was not merely progression, but two different people. Why else would David call the Christ his Lord? (Psalm 110:1) Surely he did not mean to worship himself!

The matter of Elijah and John the Baptist has been explained previously in Chapter Eleven.

Then Head and Cranston quote John 9:2, (sic 9:34).

> When there was brought into the presence of Jesus a man who was born blind, the disciples naturally wondered why he had been thus punished, and asked Jesus: 'Which did sin, this man or his parents?' The disciples must have had the idea of reincarnation in mind, for obviously if the man had been born blind, his sin could not have been committed in this life. If the doctrine was wrong and pernicious, then, it would seem, was the time for Jesus to deny the whole theory. Yet he did not do so, although in this case he said the blindness was for other reasons.[8]

The disciples may have had reincarnation in mind, since they made a lot of mistakes. But what Head and Cranston fail to mention is that Jesus did indeed deny the whole theory with one word — "neither." In the Living Bible his answer to the disciples was, "Neither,...but to demonstrate the power of God." Then he healed the man born blind, demonstrating the power of God.

Head and Cranston quote St. John in Revelation 3:12 thus: "Him that overcometh will I make a pillar in the temple of my God, and he shall go no more out." Then they say,

> Evidently he had gone out into incarnation before or the words 'no more out' could have no place or meaning. It was probably the old idea of the exile of the soul and the need for it to be purified by long wandering before it could be admitted as a 'pillar in the temple of God.'[9]

It is difficult to see how this interpretation could be more wrong. This short section of the Revelation is addressed to the church in Asia Minor which was located in the city of Philadelphia. Philadelphia was a city torn by earthquakes — very often the people had to flee to the security of the countryside. The verse quoted above would speak of permanence to them — that they will dwell safely after death once they get to the temple of God — **if** they had overcome the tendency to disbelieve in the Lord.

Another application is that the pillar in the temple is not a supporting pillar, but a monument, as is often seen in official buildings. This kind of pillar would depict the free and powerful grace of God — a monument that would never be defaced or removed. It would bear an honorable inscription (also verse 12), with "the name of my God, the city of my God and my new name." This is Christ speaking. Implied in this passage also is that the services rendered would be listed for all to see, and the name of the One under whose banner this "pillar" had served. Revelation 22:3 plainly tells of his servants, "And they shall see his face; and his name shall be in their foreheads."

Following these few wrongly interpreted Bible passages in Head and Cranston's book, there is one from the Apocrypha. The Apocrypha is not inspired by God, and is not his word.

Also included are a long list of quotations from all shades of "Christian" leaders — uninspired writings of men; all are inadmissible since they express opinions instead of the word of God.

Repeatedly, the Lord God warns us against false teachings. Below are listed some of these warnings:

> Cease, my son, to hear the instruction that causeth thee to err from the words of knowledge (Proverbs 19:27).

> Trust in the Lord with all thine heart, and lean not to thine own understanding (Proverbs 3:5).

> For there shall arise false Christs, and false prophets, and shall show great signs and wonders, insomuch that, if it were possible, they shall deceive the very elect (Matthew 24:24, Jesus speaking).

> Stop fooling yourselves. If you count yourself above average in intelligence, as judged by this world's standards, you had better put this all aside and be a fool rather than let it hold you back from the true wisdom from above. For the wisdom of this world is foolishness to God. As it says in the book of Job, God uses man's own brilliance to trap him; he stumbles over his own 'wisdom' and falls. And again, in the book of Psalms, we are told that the Lord knows full well how the human mind reasons, and how foolish and futile it is. So don't be proud of following the wise men of this world. For God has already given you everything you need (1 Corinthians 3:18-21 LB).

> Don't let others spoil your faith and joy with their philosophies, their wrong and shallow answers built on men's thoughts and ideas, instead of on what Christ has said. For in Christ there is all of God in a human body; *so you have everything when you have Christ*, and you are filled with God through your union with Christ. He is the highest Ruler, with authority over every other power (Colossians 2:8-10 LB).

> For there is going to come a time when people won't listen to the truth, but will go around looking for teachers who will tell them just what they want to hear. They won't listen to what the Bible says but will blithely follow their own misguided ideas (2 Timothy 4:4 LB).

> Avoid the godless talk and foolish arguments of 'Knowledge,' as some people wrongly call it. For some have claimed to possess it, and as a result they have lost the way of faith (1 Timothy 6:20, 21 TEV).

In 2 Timothy, Paul is warning about the difficulties of the last days. The verse which the Lord used to show me to leave a false church was 2 Timothy 3:5, "They will hold to the outward form of our religion but reject its real power. Keep away from these men (TEV)." The church I was affiliated with was religious, but the power of salvation was not taught. The people there assumed that they were saved by their presence. Never were they told that they were lost unless they made a personal decision to accept Christ as their own substitute for sin.

> It is better to trust in the Lord than to put confidence in man (Psalms 118:8).

> This is the way, walk ye in it (Isaiah 30:21). Continue in my word...and ye shall know the truth, and the truth shall make you free (Jesus, in John 8:31-32).

EIGHTEEN

Theosophy

A friend has loaned me a little book called *Heresies Exposed*, which was originally printed in 1917.[1] The chapter by A. McD. Redwood entitled "Theosophy" is of value to us. Most of the information included here on theosophy comes from this source.

Theosophy claims to be "an all-inclusive synthesis of truths, as it deals with God, the Universe, and man and their relations to each other." In the United States, the Theosophical Society was founded in 1875 by Madame Elena Petrovna Blavatsky. Hindu and Buddhist thoughts and doctrines have become largely incorporated into theosophist teachings. Among these are, particularly, reincarnation and karma.

Let us examine the beliefs of this cult:

(1). It denies the existence of a personal God. Because of this, Mrs. Annie Besant, a past leader of the group, has quoted Madame Blavatsky as saying, "Agnostics and atheists more easily assimilate theosophic teachings than do believers in orthodox creeds." This position obviously excludes the Living God of the Bible.

(2). It rejects vicarious atonement, denying altogether Christ and his work on the cross. "We believe neither in vicarious atonement, nor in the possibility of the remission of the smallest sin by any god, not even by a personal Absolute of Infinite, if such a thing could have existence," said Madame Blavatsky.

(3). It teaches reincarnation. This is called a "pivotal truth." What proof is there of reincarnation? Here is Mrs. Besant's answer: "The only proof of this doctrine...must be in the nature of things, lies for us in the future, if it exists at all."

(4). It teaches karma. It is "the twin principle of reincarnation." What does Mrs. Besant say about karma? "Even among Theosophists belief in karma is more an intellectual assent than a living fruitful conviction."

(5). Theosophy teaches about "Mahatmas," meaning "great souls." These are supposed to be exalted beings who have accumulated knowledge and wisdom over many lives. What does Mrs. Besant say of these supposed "masters of wisdom"? "Unless it is true that the soul of man comes back life after life to earth... then, indeed, the Mahatma would be an impossibility ...Reincarnation is taken for granted in the whole of this teaching." One so-called Mahatma, Koot Hoomi, wrote a letter (as an introduction to a book) which contained long extracts without acknowledgement from a speech delivered a year before by an American spiritualist. Such wisdom!

We could go on and on, building theory on top of theory, piling up castles in the air which have no foundation in fact. All of the above is poor stuff indeed to substitute for the facts of the word of God.

We might further compare the founders of these two,

Theosophy and Christianity. Madam Blavatsky was a spiritualistic medium born in Russia in 1831. She married twice; the first time to a man nearly seventy years old whom she deserted three months after marriage. Her second husband was a boy of sixteen who went mad after two days of marriage. She led a "bohemian" life and ran a gambling hall in Tiflis in 1863. Between 1848 and 1857 she claimed to visit Tibet and to have learned the secret of the Mahatmas. In 1871 Madame Blavatsky set up a spiritualistic society in Cairo. There she got into trouble for tricking the public for profit. She founded the Theosophical Society in 1875 and died in England in 1891. She wrote the book "Isis Unveiled" and experts have declared it to be filled with plagiarisms and trickery. She had a violent temper.

Now, contrast this with the divine record of the Founder of Christianity —

> Who did no sin, neither was guile found in his mouth (1 Peter 2:22).

> God anointed Jesus of Nazareth with the Holy Ghost and with power: who went about doing good, and healing all that were oppressed of the devil; for God was with him (Acts 10:38).

> Never man spake like this man (John 7:46).

And he could challenge the crowd:

> Which of you convicteth me of sin? (John 8:46):

He also could declare, sublimely and solemnly,

> I am the way, the truth, and the life.

Jesus' enemies could find little to accuse him of: (1) He performed miracles on the Sabbath day, and (2) he claimed to be God in the flesh. If he was **not** God in the flesh, there are only two possibilities: if he knew it to be untrue, he was a liar; if he did not know it to be untrue, he was a lunatic. But if his claim to be God is fact, then all he did was tell the truth; and he is Lord. Liar, lunatic, Lord: take your choice. C. S. Lewis rightly argues that these are the only three alternatives open to us.[2]

C. S. Lewis continues,

> You can shut Him up for a fool, you can spit at Him and kill Him as a demon; or you can fall at His feet and call Him Lord and God. But let us not come up with any patronizing nonsense about His being a great human teacher. He has not left that open to us. He did not intend to.[2]

Author John Phillips authenticates Jesus as follows:

> One chance in 537 million! The prophets who made [Bible] predictions lived at different times. Their viewpoints differed; their temperament, circumstances, and modes of expression were not the same. Their prophetic vision, however, was uniformly focused mainly on one of two great future events — the first and second comings of Christ. Each gave a little more light until, putting all their glimmering candles together, we have a blazing nova beam. One of the great focal points of Old Testament prophecy was an event the prophets themselves did not understand — the crucifixion of Israel's Messiah.
>
> In one twenty-four hour period at least twenty-nine [Old Testament] prophecies concerning Christ's death were literally fulfilled. Here are some of them [first the ancient prophecy; then the fulfilled reality in Jesus' life]:
>
> He was to be sold for thirty pieces of silver (Zechariah 11:2, fulfilled in Matthew 26:14-15); betrayed by a friend (Psalms 55:12-14, 41:9; Matthew 26:47-50); accused by false witnesses (Psalms 35:11, 109:2; Matthew 26:59-60);

smitten and spit upon in the face (Isaiah 50:6, Luke 22:64, Matthew 26:67-68); silent before his accusers (Isaiah 53:7, Matthew 27:12-14); pierced in both hands and feet (Psalms 22:16, Luke 23:33); ridiculed (Psalms 22:8, Matthew 27:41-43); forsaken by God (Psalms 22:1, Matthew 27:46); given vinegar and gall to drink (Psalms 69:21, Matthew 27:34, John 19:28-29); protected from having His bones broken, [Psalms 34:20] (Psalms 22:14, 17; John 19:31-36); pierced in the side (Zechariah 12:10, John 19:34-37); buried in a rich man's tomb (Isaiah 53:9, Matthew 27:57-60).

According to the law of compound probabilities, the chance that these twenty-nine prophecies could have been so literally fulfilled by accident is one in 537 million.[3]

There's quite a contrast between Jesus Christ and everyone else!

Can a Christian be a Theosophist? Mrs. Besant says YES:

No man in becoming a Theosophist, need cease to be a Christian, a Buddhist, a Hindu; he will but acquire a deeper insight into his own faith.[4]

Can a Christian become a Theosophist? The Bible says NO:

Don't be teamed with those who do not love the Lord, for what do the people of God have in common with the people of sin? How can light live with darkness? And what harmony can there be between Christ and the devil? How can a Christian be a partner with one who doesn't believe? And what union can there be between God's temple and idols?...the Lord has said, 'Leave them; separate yourselves from them; don't touch their filthy things.' (2 Corinthians 6:14-17 LB)

> Christianity is the final religion. Christ himself is God's last word. The Theosophists are looking for a greater, but we know from the New Testament that a greater need not be expected. The Christ has come. I speak quite reverently when I say that God has exhausted his vocabulary. He has spoken His last word. If there is any hope for the world, it is to be found in Christ. If it cannot be found in Christ, it cannot be found at all.[5]
>
> St. Paul, the servant of God, wrote:
>
> Let God's curses fall on anyone, including myself, who preaches any other way to be saved than the one we told you about; yes, if an angel comes from heaven and preaches any other message, let him be forever cursed. I will say it again: if anyone preaches any other Gospel than the one you welcomed, let God's curse fall upon him (Galatians 1:8,9 LB).

Reincarnation, karma, Theosophy, etc., are all "other gospels."

How can we tell a true gospel from a false one? The test is grace, which is **God's unmerited favor**. If the teaching excludes grace, or mixes it with works as a way to be either saved or forgiven, it is another gospel. Anyone teaching or believing another gospel is under God's curse.

If this sounds narrow-minded, please address your complaints to God. Jesus said it was a narrow way, and few would find it. He himself is that way.

I once heard a reincarnationist give such a garbled definition of "grace" that I could scarcely believe my own ears. Let no one deceive you — most simply stated grace is **God's unmerited favor**. It takes a while for the impact of those three little words to soak in. That grace of God is found only through Jesus Christ — "grace and truth came by Jesus Christ (John 1:17)."

In order to be part of the human race, we must have human parents, and be physically born. In order to be part of the kingdom of God, we must have a personal, indwelling relationship with his Son. It is the only way to be reborn, and the only way to receive God's grace. In either case, birth is the first step. And birth is essential. Without birth, the physical life does not exist. Without Christian rebirth, the spiritual life does not exist.

The Theosophical Society aims "to form a nucleus of the Universal Brotherhood of Humanity, without distinction of race, creed, sex, caste, or color." They lecture it, but do they live it? A woman who was a member of that group says they don't. She also says,

> Suddenly, I realized that Theosophy offered plausible theories but no power.It supplied seemingly rational concepts of life, but no strength for everyday living.[6,7]

In answer to human misery, Theosophy has this to offer: "It must be your karma; you probably deserve it." But Jesus says, "I came that they might have life, and that they might have it more abundantly (John 10:10)." "If the Son, therefore, shall set you free, ye shall be free indeed (John 8:36)."

NINETEEN

Shirley MacLaine and Company

Movie star Shirley MacLaine is now an outspoken supporter of reincarnationist views in books, lectures and television. She speaks as one who has had experiences, conversations and insights leading her to her conclusions. As such, she has captured the attention of the American public as only a celebrity can. She has also aligned herself with "New Age" thought, going far beyond reincarnation and karma and into other occult fields.

Many of the beliefs that Shirley MacLaine espouses have been dealt with throughout this book. I want to point out here that "trance channelling" is merely a new name for mediumship. The Bible never denies that contact with the spirit world is possible. In fact, we are urged to recognize the reality of the spiritual realm, and the two real opposing forces there. The Bible urges us to pray to God in Jesus' name and to flee from Satan and his deceptions. It is phenomenally dangerous to accept as good and true whatever is said "spiritually."

John the Beloved says:

> My dear friends, do not believe all who claim to have the Spirit, but test them to find out if the spirit they have comes from God. For many false prophets have gone out everywhere. This is how you will be able to know whether it is God's Spirit: anyone who acknowledges that Jesus Christ came as a human being has the Spirit who comes from God. But anyone who denies this about Jesus does not have the Spirit from God. The spirit that he has is from the Enemy of Christ; you heard that it would come, and now it is here in the world already (1 John 4:1-3 TEV).

Shirley MacLaine tells of "Astral" guides who lead her. But Jesus said it is the "Spirit of Truth" (the Holy Spirit) who will guide you into all truth. (John 16:13) There are evil spirits and they are not truthful. They use whatever means they can to deceive you. Naturally, if they can reach a naive listener, they will pose as wise, all knowing, authoritative kindly mentors. If you are communicating with a spirit, add to the "fun and games" by asking whether Jesus Christ came as a human being and insist on a plain answer. And, whether you are paying or not, it would be interesting to ask why no spirit ever describes a former life as a born-again Christian, filled with the Holy Spirit of God. Another interesting question would be if Jesus Christ had been truly raised from the dead.

According to the Bible, God did raise Jesus Christ from the dead. Because he did that, God can also raise up his other children from the dead, as he has promised to do. Like Jesus, our bodies will be intact, but different (see Chapter Seven). If the body were unimportant, God would not have promised to resurrect it as he has over and over again in the Bible, and demonstrated in the case of Jesus Christ. This one lifetime is crucial to our eternal existence. The Bible teaches us that unless we reconcile with God the Father in this life, we forever forfeit the opportunity to do so.

God originally made man in his image, as complete as he is. When sin entered, the spiritual part of our perfection died. Without the new birth, no matter how hard we try, the imperfection persists and we long to be god-like. The "New Age" movement uses this instinctive desire for god-like qualities to try to substitute their way for God's way. But the only real way to incorporate divinity is by simply asking the true God to dwell within. As Jesus Christ legally enters through our will and choice, the divine is restored and completion finally occurs.

"Therefore, if any man be in Christ, he is a new creature: old things are passed away; behold, all things are become new (2 Cor. 5:17)." In this way we become "partakers of the divine nature (2 Peter 1:4)," "And ye are complete in him, which is the head of all principality and power (Col. 2:10)."

But man is **NOT** God even then, and to claim "I am God" as New Agers tell us to do is to utter blasphemy. It's the same old lie that Satan whispered to Eve. "Ye shall be as gods (Genesis 3:4)." No difference. It did not work for Eve and it will not work for us.

If a person believes he or she is a god, arrogance and tyranny must be the result. Many dysfunctional families are or were ruled by such a person. Havoc is the natural result, as all family members must adapt in some way to the dictates of the "god." Even Edgar Cayce decried this delusion. He is quoted as saying, "What caused the first influences in the earth that brought selfishness? The desire to be as gods, in that rebellion became the order of the mental forces in the soul; and sin entered."[1] Imagine if **each** person thinks themself a god, each one demanding their own way, with no Supreme Perfect God to answer to, no standard except their own!

No one wants to be a loser. A careful study of Christianity and reincarnation reveals the truth — if either one is right, the other is wrong. They cannot both be right. If a person chooses Jesus Christ, and if reincarnation is true, they've gained a lot of good karma to show for this lifetime. But if Christianity is right, the reincarnationist has gambled and lost it all, and that forever.

> In the world to come for those who believe in reincarnation, there is only more disease, more destruction, and more death. In the world to come for the children of God, there will be no more suffering, and the lion will lie down at peace with the lamb.[2]

Which gives more hope: the positive assurance of Christ within or vague nebulous questions of karmic retribution or reward?

Christians are sometimes accused of "pie-in-the-sky-someday-bye-and-bye" thinking. But the Bible says emphatically: "Now is the accepted time; behold, now is the day of salvation (2 Corinthians 6:2)." Belief in reincarnation and karma is far more pie-in-the-sky than that!

Jesus' love, mercy, honesty and dedication to his mission were obvious to everyone who met him. The Bible says:

> ...grace...has been revealed to us through the coming of our Savior, Christ Jesus. He has ended the power of death and through the gospel has revealed immortal life (2 Tim. 1:9-10 TEV).

> "With all their seemingly 'good' emphases, the New Age Movement is at heart humanistic (man is the center of the universe), materialistic (self-actualization is all-important), and anti-God (the God of the Bible is

dismissed in favor of self-deification). The American public, with its inability to distinguish biblical truth from anti-Christian religious subtleties, is easily sucked in by the seemingly harmless religious and cultural goals of New Age humanism."[3]

Since most of us don't recognize Hinduism or witchcraft, few protest. From teachers causing children to visualize a "wise person" instructing them, to movies with beloved old George Burns and Lucas thrillers; witchcraft and Hinduism, by subterfuge, are being imprinted on our whole society. Shirley MacLaine is only one of the most visible Americans leading us away from Biblical truth.

Many parents have no idea what television, music, teachers or textbooks are teaching their children. Although some influences are positive, many are not. See Texe Marrs' eye-popping chapter, "Cry For Our Children,"[4] and Dave Hunt's revealing section "Truth or Lie?"[5]. Educators using "confluent education," "values clarification" and "enlightenment" are spiritually abusing our children at taxpayers' expense.

Judy Price is CBS' vice-president for children's television programming.

> When stating why she got involved in children's programming, Price said it was because she could get more controversial subject matter past the network censors than with adult programming. Quoting Price: 'I could get away with more...I think we've broken a lot of ground where people would not have dared to go in prime time.'[6]

It makes one wonder — get away with what? Who is "we"? Just what ground have they broken? How much influence do they have? Do they care about the children?

Shirley MacLaine — beautiful, talented, famous, charming, intelligent and compassionate. How she will weep when she sees how she has been used like the Pied Piper to lure many trusting souls into deception and destruction!

WHICH?

We read God's Word,
We read MacLaine.
The fact absurd
It is so plain.
Crystal clear it is to see
That they distinctly disagree.
The question (tho' it may seem odd):
Who is right? MacLaine or God?

Shirley MacLaine believes that nothing happens by accident, and that every little thing serves a purpose of some kind, however obscure. Unlike her, I believe that we live in a natural world where accidents can happen, quite apart from God's will. I believe that God respects the laws of nature which he devised, and will only interfere with them at the direct, specific, believing request of his children. This is one purpose of prayer.

I have come to see that most "bad things" are caused directly or indirectly by the selfishness and sin of people. Knowing God's character proves that these are not his will.

Sometimes people think that if God does something for you on one hand, he'll "zap" you with the other. Again, knowing God's character proves this is not true. Proverbs 10:22 says, "The blessing of the Lord, it maketh rich, and he addeth no sorrow with it." How long do his blessings last? Read Psalm 136. "His mercy endureth forever" is repeated 26 times just in this one place.

Experience over recent years has proved to me that tragedy can strike anyone including me. I have learned that as I trust God in any situation, he will not only walk through it with me, but will inevitably, **always** turn it to good!

God calls death our "last enemy." He turns even that to good by means of resurrecting his children. He will give us a glorified version of the mortal body: his perfect character guarantees his word of honor. Jesus Christ was the first to receive this glorified kind of body (Luke 24:36-43, John 20:26-29). The enemies of Jesus made very sure that he was really dead (John 19:33,34 and Mark 15:44,45). They were careful to have Roman soldiers guard his tomb (Matthew 27:62-66). But he arose from the dead the third day as he had promised (Matthew 28, Mark 16, Luke 24, John 20). How they must have searched for the body! How angry they must have been to hear reports of so many people who had seen him alive. How frustrated they were that the tomb where Jesus had laid was empty — empty. No matter how they tried, the tomb was empty, the body never found, the disciples of Jesus absolutely revolutionized! (Acts 2,3, and 4)

> The last enemy that shall be destroyed is death. It [Our flesh] is sown in corruption; it is raised in incorruption. It is sown in dishonor; it is raised in glory. It is sown in weakness; it is raised in power. It is sown a natural body; it is raised a spiritual body....For this corruptible must put on incorruption, and this mortal must put on immortality. Then...Death is swallowed up in victory...Thanks be to God, who giveth us the victory through our Lord Jesus Christ (1 Corinthians 15:26, 42-44, 57).

What a wonderful and certain hope that resurrection is! And how do we get that resurrection? Jesus Christ said,

> "I am the resurrection, and the life; he that believeth in me, though he were dead, yet shall he live. And whosoever liveth and believeth in me shall never die. Believest thou this?" (John 11:25-26)

Believest thou this?

TWENTY

Rainbows and Swastikas

It seemed then that the "flower children" of the sixties were harmless and sweet, and maybe they were. Until two months before press time, I thought the same about New Age people. I still think the vast majority of New Agers are like me, longing for peace and love in the world and wanting someone to fix it. The threat of nuclear war hangs over us all. Many have lost control of their lives and are desperately searching for help. Presented with "relaxation," "meditation" and hopes for inner and world peace, they are ripe for those who would exploit their needs. The "other" control can seem wise and helpful. We live, unfortunately, in perilous times. Most New Age adherents are in for a terrible shock when they see what they have really supported. Astrology is the basis of new age thought.

Who are New Agers? Basically, they are searchers, intelligent people who have the vision to see that there is more to life than the daily grind. They see the beauty in nature and are sensitive to the evils around us. They may have had innoculative doses of false Christianity (see Chapter 13), and know that that can't be all there is. They want to make a difference. They come from all strata of society, but tend to be the better educated. They can be overly self-involved and mystical, and most believe that man is innately good instead of sinful.

I don't claim to be an expert on the New Age movement, but others are. My purpose here is a warning and a plea to find out what the experts and New Age writers themselves are saying. Look behind the froth and learn what "The Plan" is all about and how widespread and sinister it really is. "The Plan" is written out on pages 15-17 of *Dark Secrets of the New Age.*[1]

According to some people, "The Age of Aquarius" is upon us. New Agers claim that the old age of Pisces is disappearing and that those who refuse or cannot make the change will not be suitable for the New Age. This New Age, they say, calls for one world government using one financial system, and one world religion, united under one world ruler. Adherents believe that their involvement is important in order to usher in world peace and prosperity under this system. The appeal of the religious ideas they put forth is that whatever religion anyone chooses is perfectly acceptable — unless, of course, one happens to believe in One God, and/or only one path to him (i.e., Jews, Christians, and some Moslems). Such people are classified as "separatist" and "divisionary," and are expendable. In fact, New Age writers teach that those who believe in One God cannot be happy here in this world and should be "released" from this life to find a happier reincarnation elsewhere. (No, I am not making this up.) See *Dark Secrets of the New Age*[2], *Hidden Dangers of the Rainbow*[3], and *Peace, Prosperity and the Coming Holocaust*[4], and their **extensive bibliographies** of New Age writings.

In *Dark Secrets of the New Age*, Texe Marrs cites 600 quotes from New Age leaders. Their "Plan," besides establishment of one world government and one world religion, is to eliminate every trace of Christianity and Judaism. On the back cover, Marrs' book claims to show:

> "...exactly what is now being done by the New Age leadership to gain influence in every facet of society, from the entertainment industry to public schools and government. Marrs details specifically the New Age Plan to win over the next generation by flooding the media — TV cartoon shows, movies, comic books, libraries, etc. — with material that promotes New Age religious thinking and doctrine. Finally, Marrs shows how New Age ideas have already begun to infiltrate and undermine Christian churches from within.[6]"

Very recently, I unsuspectingly attended a seminar aimed at "healing the child within." At one point, a tape was played in which music and a speaker used imagery to get those present out of the body to a different plane of existence. I refused to participate since I know what a trap hypnosis is, but all around me others were going into a trance. How subtle it was! I was very "separatist" indeed as I willed not to submit my mind to unknown forces. I was the only one present of about one hundred people who resisted the takeover!

In a newspaper article discussing cults, Diane Salvatore says, "New Age blends Eastern and Western thought and encompasses self-help groups, healing crystals, reincarnation and channeling." She quotes Reginald Alev of the Cult Awareness Network in Chicago as saying that the New Age phenomenon, particularly channeling, shares characteristics with destructive cults. Alev says, "Many followers are addicted to a hypnotic subculture." Salvatore quotes Phillip Abramowitz, director of the Task Force on Missionaries and Cults of the Jewish Community Relations Council of New York: "Literally millions of dollars are given to cults by people who are told they will be taught to communicate with those they leave behind when they die.[7]"

Only Jesus truly spoke to the dead. When he said, "Lazarus, come forth," Lazarus came forth alive (John 11:43,44).

New Age adherents are preparing the way for the "Lord," the "Christ of the New Age," they say. Benjamin Creme, New Age spokesman, names this "Lord" as "Maitreya."[8,9] People involved in the New Age movement frequently hear a call for "the Christ" to "return." They should not be deceived: it is not Jesus Christ, but "Maitreya" (or the fifth Buddha, or Krishna, or Iman Mahdi) or many other "gods" they are invoking. Contrary to New Age claims[10], this is **not** a person known to Christians as Jesus Christ nor to Jews as Messiah.[11] New Age theory is that Jesus was Lord and Christ for the Old Age, but not for the New one.[12] Some worship "Maitreya" in the mistaken belief that he is the most recent and most advanced reincarnation of the Christ.[13] The Bible, however, says, "Jesus Christ, the same yesterday, and today, and forever (Hebrews 13:8)."

Benjamin Creme states that the New Age christ is already living.[14] Jesus Christ said, "Then if any man shall say unto you, Lo, here is Christ, or there; believe it not (Matthew 24:23ff)."

The man Creme speaks of could be the one the Bible warns us will come, the antichrist himself. He will pose as a man of peace (Revelation 13:11). Revelation 13 tells us much about this man. He will make war with the saints. Power will be given to him over all kindreds, and tongues and nations. (The New Age movement has thousands of organizations worldwide, and is gathering strength.[15]) The antichrist will have power as prophesied for seven years. No one will be able to buy or sell anything unless they accept his "mark", his rulership and his system (Revelation 13:16-18). He will also fall as prophesied after seven years (Revelation 13:5, Revelation 19:20).

New Age mentors teach evolution.[16] Physical evolution of humans explains away God the Creator to whom we must answer. "Spiritual evolution" through reincarnation will be used to justify a "master race." Those who have "evolved spiritually" through many reincarnations are thought to be clearly superior to others.[17,18] (Again, please check those bibliographies!)

Speaking of a "master race," Hitler thought he was founding a reign of 1000 years. An ominous parallel is shown between Nazism and the New Age movement in *Hidden Dangers of the Rainbow*.[19] Constance Cumbey's list goes on for several pages (pages 114-120). She recommends the book, *The Occult and the Third Reich*.[20]

It is most ironic that anyone who is Jewish would support the New Age movement.[21] Their cry is "Never again!," when reminded of the Holocaust.[22] Yet several times in the last few years there have been outrageous claims that the Holocaust "never happened" or was "exaggerated." This despite the fact of many survivors, pictures, remaining sites and much proof of it. That big lie has already started, only forty years later. Hitler's tactics are being duplicated as society kills first the most helpless; the unborn, the unwanted, the deformed or retarded, the critically ill. More than 20 million unborn have died "legally" in America alone since 1973. Pretending people are sub-human is still used as an excuse to kill them. Hitler called the killing of the Jews a "cleansing action" which is exactly the term and solution New Age writers are calling for when they have the power; "cleansing the earth" not only of Jews, but anyone who resists their system.[23]

The resemblance between New Age teaching and that of Nazism is not accidental. Both of these, and many pagan religions, are based on the Babylonian Mystery religions. These featured worship of many gods, or self as god, or god as a "force" rather than a person; communication with "the dead";

"Masters of Wisdom" (found through trance); belief in and practice of sorcery or magic; reincarnation and karma; progressive secret initiation rites and oaths[24]; exaltation of earth, moon, sun and stars; astrology; use of drugs and witchcraft, chanting and calling on demonic names; devaluation of human life; and "special" knowledge. Also, they feature a drive for "unity" as evidenced in the "Tower of Babel (Genesis 11)."[25] The religion of the builders of Babel lives on in Masonic and other teachings.[26]

As discussed earlier, all worship and praise not specifically directed to the true and Living God goes to Satan. Regardless of the intent, that "father of lies," that thief Satan, appropriates the worship as unto himself, the god of this world. So nothing is really changed from the Babylonian Mystery religions. It need not be changed much since it still does what it always has; rob God of his rightful place in the hearts and minds of people, doom those people and instill worship of Satan.

Most people involved in the New Age movement are truly yearning for what is good and right; peace on earth, an end to suffering and hunger, and love extended to all. It sounds so nice, and the symbolic rainbow so lovely. Then, too, most do not know enough about the Bible to see the red flags or to realize what is really happening. They forget that when the kingdom of God is made manifest, all WILL be perfect (Revelation 21).

Before the kingdom of God reigns on earth, as the power of the New Age movement and its veiled Hinduism continues to grow, and before the antichrist has the power he seeks, the world may find a short time of seeming peace and prosperity. During this period there would be no universal acceptance of a strong world ruler since things would already be working so well. But unexpectedly at some instant in the future, every born-again Christian believer in the world will suddenly vanish.

Jesus said, "One will be taken, and one will be left (Matthew 24:40-44)."

> Now this I say, brethren, that flesh and blood cannot inherit the kingdom of God; neither doth corruption inherit incorruption. Behold, I shew you a mystery: We shall not all sleep, but we shall all be changed. In a moment, in the twinkling of an eye, at the last trump: for the trumpet shall sound, and the dead shall be raised incorruptible, and we shall be changed (1 Corinthians 15:50-52).

> For this we say unto you by the word of the Lord, that we who are alive and remain unto the coming of the Lord shall not precede them who are asleep. For the Lord himself shall descend from heaven with a shout, with the voice of the archangel, and with the trump of God; and the dead in Christ shall rise first: Then we who are alive and remain shall be caught up together with them in the clouds, to meet the Lord in the air; and so shall we ever be with the Lord. Wherefore, comfort one another with these words (1 Thessalonians 4:15-18).

Bible believing Christians have long expected this amazing event, called "The Rapture." Although the shock of it will be world-wide, America is virtually the only nation in the world with vast numbers of Christians in every strata of society. America's political, financial, transportation, communication and other structures would fall in that "twinkling of an eye." The resulting world-wide chaos and terror for those left behind would open wide the gates for the antichrist to take over. For years, New Age leaders have been accumulating demonic predictions of a "quantum leap" for New Agers, complete with a new name, "Homo Noeticus."[27] (The dictionary says noetic means relating to or based on a purely intellectual apprehension.[28] In other words, excluding God.) Texe Marrs refers to this "leap" also, mentioning New Ager's theory of "transformational evolution," by which a "critical mass" of energy exuding from many racially superior beings will bring a new "Cosmic Consciousness."[29] The people then would be told that since Christians were unfit for the New Age, they have been removed by God or a Force in the interests of the "Spiritual Evolution" of the New Age. For more information on this whole "contrary scenario," I strongly recommend *Peace, Prosperity and the Coming Holocaust*, by Dave Hunt.[30]

No one but God knows exactly when the Rapture will occur. Some Christians, like Hunt, believe it will be before the "Great Tribulation." Others, hoping "pre-tribs" are right, think it will be either during or after the seven year reign of antichrist. Whoever is right, no matter what Satan or anyone else plans, God will have his way at the time he chooses. He merely tells Christians to watch, pray and be ready.

Bible prophecies written thousands of years ago are being fulfilled in our time, including the political reestablishment of the nation of Israel and Jewish possession of Jerusalem. Every single Bible prophecy will come to pass.[31] For a vivid 2000 year old description of the final world religion (the New Age Movement?), see Revelation 17. There John the Beloved saw a woman in a vision:

> ...I saw a woman sit upon a scarlet-colored beast, full of names of blasphemy, having seven heads and ten horns. And the woman was arrayed in purple and scarlet color, and bedecked with gold and precious stones and pearls, having a golden cup in her hand, full of abominations and filthiness of her fornication; And upon her forehead was a name written, MYSTERY, BABYLON THE GREAT, THE MOTHER OF HARLOTS AND ABOMINATIONS

> OF THE EARTH. And I saw the woman drunk with the blood of the saints, and with the blood of the martyrs of Jesus; and when I saw her, I wondered with great wonder (Revelation 17:3-6).

Verse 15 explains "the waters thou sawest, where the harlot sitteth, are peoples, and multitudes, and nations and tongues." In other words a false religion, "Mystery, Babylon the Great," which like a harlot perverts true worship, will rule over many kinds of people. This religion is so unified that it is one harlot. Rich and powerful and merciless, this religion is so unified as to be called one person, a harlot.

This shows again how desperate Satan is to pervert and counterfeit all that God does. Peter tells us of God's plan to unify **his** people, and tells who God's people are (1 Peter 1:2). Revelation 21 describes the "Bride of Christ," the holy city, the New Jerusalem; the unity of God's people. Note that they are so united as to be referred to as one woman, chaste and pure, a bride. Satan's "unity," the harlot, is a perversion of God's plan.

The Bible says of the "kings" of the beast (those who rule under antichrist):

> These have one mind, and shall give their power and strength unto the beast. These shall make war with the Lamb, and the Lamb shall overcome them; for he is Lord of lords, and King of kings, and they that are with him are called, and chosen, and faithful (Revelation 17:13,14).

The counterfeit religion of Satan will fall, destroyed by the beast (the antichrist) whom she thinks she rules (Revelation 17:16). Chapter 18 of Revelation describes this as the fall of Babylon. Revelation 19:20, 21 tells the fate of the antichrist (the world ruler, the beast), the false prophet (the head of the harlot religion), and their followers. The destruction of the antichrist and the false prophet ends two-thirds of the unholy trinity. Satan will be bound while Jesus Christ and his people reign on the earth for 1,000 years (Revelation 20:1-6). When Satan is released for a while, he will again gather followers for one last battle. Finally, he will be destroyed also (Revelation 20:10). Then comes judgment day for every person of every age who has rejected Jesus Christ (Revelation 20:11-15). Revelation 22:1-5 tells what happens to the people of God. It says, in part: "...and they shall reign forever and ever (Revelation 22:5)."

Those who love God and his only begotten Son should have no fear. Jesus said, "Be of good cheer. I have overcome the world (John 16:33)." The coming storm only proves that Bible prophecies are true.

Christians have a perfect blueprint to follow in the time to come, laid out for us in Ephesians 6:10-18 and Acts, chapters one through four. The power, anointing, love and discernment of the Holy Spirit are ours. We are more than conquerers! (Romans 8:37)

Jesus Christ is the Rock of Ages — all ages. Astrological "ages", parapsychology, self as god, monism, (all-is-one,) pantheism, gnosticism, secular humanism and all that go with them are lies. The New Age is a lie. But the heart of God is yearning for each of us to repent and to have a personal relationship with him through his only Son, Jesus Christ. This is the gospel truth.

TWENTY-ONE

Personal Testimony — The Way Out

The deception of reincarnation nearly destroyed me, and through me, our family. The very nature of deception is that it seems harmless, innocent and acceptable. It's hard to believe that there was a way out, and looking back, I can see that only by the grace of God has it happened. Jesus promises, "...the Son abideth forever. If the Son therefore, shall make you free, ye shall be free indeed (John 8:36)." I testify that the Son of God has indeed set me free from the bondage of deception.

Jesus has divine purpose in setting us free. He urges us then, "Be ye perfect (Matthew 5:48)," meaning to grow up, become mature. This is a lifelong process. As far as I can tell, we never become perfect in earthly life. But we can get closer. Closer by consciously seeking: (1) to please the Lord, and (2) his direction for our lives. Closer, by regular attendance at a church where the entire Bible is believed and faithfully taught. Closer, by consistent prayer and private Bible study. Closer, by loving others in our own power and by also letting Jesus love them through us. Closer, by praising him in **all** circumstances; since trust is strengthened by exercise. It is **eternally** worth the effort!

The process of coming closer and closer to God is called a "walk." The term is used very often in the scriptures, such as Isaiah 2:5, "Let us walk in the light of the Lord;" and 2 Corinthians 5:7, "For we walk by faith, not by sight." My Bible concordance has an entire column of references to this step-by-step progression.

It is heartening to know that the perfect life of Christ is imputed to us the moment we believe. His perfection is laid to our account so that in the sight of God we **are** perfect; the indwelling perfection of Christ makes it so!

Ever since I could remember, I had yearned for a lifetime goal worth reaching. For a long time I settled for the aim to be a good wife and mother. But even that failed to permanently satisfy. Now, at last I have found a goal which satisfies completely. My desire is to fit the pattern NOW that God had for me from the beginning. Every Christian is meant to be a unique facet reflecting that particular beauty of God which only he or she can. To do that, simply that, gives identity and meaning to life, and deep down satisfaction. The searching stops — the yearning ends, identity and purpose are at last resolved. Growth begins. The mind gradually becomes renewed.

Only recently have I fully understood a little song I wrote years ago:

> See the moon. It pictures Christians.
> Reflecting light which is the Son's.
> Drawing tides of people to him,
> Shining love on everyone.

I needed the sixteen years between the start and publication of this book to mature and grow spiritually, and to cultivate the serenity which Jesus referred to as peace. He said in John 14:27,

> Peace I leave with you, my peace I give unto you; not as the world giveth, give I unto you. Let not your heart be troubled, neither let it be afraid.

That peace is inner harmony which results from learning who God is, asking him to dwell within, and knowing who we are; doing these things results in living a life suitable to Christ. That suitable life is not so much **doing** as **being**; resting in him (Matthew 11:28,29).

The gift of God is eternal life. It began with my rebirth and shall continue forever. Thanks be to God, I am a spirit, I have a soul, I live presently in a body. All three me; all three unique; and all three valuable — to be united again as one at the resurrection. Transformed, yet the same person.

The Fortieth Psalm has become my praise to God, particularly the first few verses:

> I waited patiently for the LORD, and he inclined unto me, and heard my cry. He brought me up also out of an horrible pit, out of the miry clay, and set my feet upon a rock, and established my goings. And he hath put a new song in my mouth, even praise unto our God; many shall see it, and fear, and shall trust in the LORD. Blessed is that man who maketh the LORD his trust, and respecteth not the proud, nor such as turn aside to lies. Many, O LORD my God, are thy wonderful works which thou hast done, and thy thoughts which are toward us; they cannot be reckoned up in order unto thee: If I would declare and speak of them, they are more than can be numbered....I delight to do thy will, O my God; yea, thy law is within my heart... But I am poor and needy; yet the LORD thinketh upon me (Psalm 40:1-5,8,17).

One of the most beautiful aspects of the new birth is the arrival of joy. Joy and happiness are actually contrasts;

happiness depends on "happenings" and circumstances. But joy is deeper and bubbles within regardless of the circumstances, since it reflects the finality of peace with God. Peace, joy and love do indeed go together. Someone has said that the formula for joy is as follows:

Jesus first; **O**thers second; **Y**ourself last = **JOY**.

It's true! It was a great day for me when I gave up the pursuit of happiness for the acceptance of joy. Millions of others can testify to the same.

There's a "Great Day" coming for us all. Every knee shall bow and every tongue confess that Jesus Christ is Lord. And we shall all see him face to face.

It is my prayer that you, whoever you are, whatever your problems may be, will find the ultimate answer in Jesus Christ. He is the way, the truth and the life. No one comes to the Father but by him.

> For salvation that comes from trusting Christ — which is what we preach — is already within easy reach of each of us; in fact, it is as near as our own hearts and mouths. For if you tell others with your own mouth that Jesus Christ is your Lord, and believe in your own heart that God has raised him from the dead, you will be saved. For it is believing in his heart that a man becomes right with God; and with his mouth he tells others of his faith, confirming his salvation. For the Scriptures tell us that no one who believes in Christ will ever be disappointed... Anyone who calls upon the name of the Lord will be saved (Romans 10:8-11 LB).

It must be in **this** life! After death is too late.
"Behold, now is the accepted time; behold, now is the day of salvation (2 Corinthians 6:2)."

Maybe I was reborn with that one-word prayer, "Help!" but once I understood how vital the rebirth is, I was taking no chances. So I prayed a simple prayer much like the one on the following page actually requesting the Lord Jesus to enter my heart and life. If you're not sure of your standing, I hope you will use it. But, I urge you not to ask Jesus in as Savior (insurance policy) only. He must also be invited in as Lord (Master). When you find yourself willing to change toward his plan for you, you can be sure that **your** ordinary miracle has occurred! Jesus said, "Follow me." The truly reborn person **wants** to obey that order, regardless of cost.

If the Lord has chosen to use my past foolishness to bring just one person to himself, then I say, "Hallelujah!" May all the glory go to God. He is the only one worthy to receive it.

Heavenly Father, I thank you for showing me the true way to be acceptable in your sight. I renounce all false beliefs and teachings. I confess all sins and ask for cleansing through the finished work of Jesus Christ. I accept you, Jesus, as my personal and only Savior. I accept you as Lord of my life. Take it and use it as you will. I ask you now to come into my heart and give me eternal life. I am not worthy of it, but I thank you for it. Keep drawing me closer to yourself, Oh Lord. Teach me the truth of the Bible and give me a hunger for it. Fill me with your Holy Spirit. Grant me the assurance of the truth of your promises...I pray with thanksgiving in Jesus' name. AMEN.

Apostle's Creed

I believe in God the Father Almighty, Maker of heaven and earth: and in Jesus Christ His only Son our Lord, Who was conceived by the Holy Ghost, born of the Virgin Mary, suffered under Pontius Pilate, was crucified, dead, and buried: He descended into hell; on the third day He arose again from the dead; He ascended into heaven, and sitteth on the right hand of God the Father Almighty; from thence He shall come to judge the quick and the dead.

I believe in the Holy Ghost; the holy Christian church, the communion of saints; the forgiveness of sins; the resurrection of the body, and the life everlasting.

Amen.

NOTES

Chapter One: BEGINNINGS, RATIONALE

1. Josh McDowell, *Evidence that Demands A Verdict*, (Arrowhead Springs, CA: Campus Crusade for Christ, 1972).
2. Paul E. Little, *Know Why You Believe*, (Wheaton, IL: Scripture Press Publications, 1967).
3. S. I. McMillen, M. D., *None of These Diseases*, (Old Tappan, NJ: Spire Books, 1963).
4. M. R. DeHaan, M. D., *The Tabernacle*, (Grand Rapids, MI: Zondervan, 1979).
5. Barry Wood, *Questions New Christians Ask*, (Old Tappan, NJ: Fleming Revell, 1979).

Chapter Two:
REBIRTH, UNIVERSAL FATHERHOOD OF GOD

1. See also: Matthew 13:37-43; Galatians 4:5; Ephesians 1:5; Hosea 2:23; Romans 8:9; Romans 8:14; 2 Corinthians 6:14-18; 1 John 3:1-4; 7-13.

Chapter Three: ANIMAL SOULS? SPIRIT, SOUL, BODY

1. Dean Barton, in a speech at Faith Baptist Church, Wilmington, Delaware, 1974.

2. Watchman Nee, *The Spiritual Man*, Volume 1, Combined Edition, (NY: Christian Fellowship Publishers, 1977) pgs. 21,23,28.

Chapter Five: KARMA, JUSTICE, PERSONAL GOD

1. Robert Lowry, *Nothing But The Blood*, A Hymn, Public Domain.

Recommended Reading:

* H. Clay Trumbull, *The Blood Covenant*, (Kirkwood, MO: Impact Books, 1975).
* Leon Morris, *The Atonement*, (Leicester, England: Intervarsity Press, 1983).

Chapter Six: NATURAL, CARNAL, SPIRITUAL

1. C. S. Lovett, *Why Die As You Are!*, (Baldwin Park, CA: Personal Christianity, 1969). Now titled *Jesus Is Coming -Get Ready Christian!*
2. Dick Hillis, *Are the Heathen Really Lost?*, (Chicago: Moody Press).
3. Dr. J. B. Williams, in a sermon at Faith Baptist Church Wilmington, Delaware, 1974.

Chapter Eight: SECOND CHANCE? DEATH, SPIRITUAL

1. Don Basham, *True and False Prophets*, (Greensburg, PA: Manna Books, 1973).

Chapter Nine: DEATH, PHYSICAL

1. C. I. Scofield, D. D., Editor, *The New Scofield Reference Bible*, (NY: Oxford University Press, 1967), p. 1319.
2. John Newton, Amazing Grace, A Hymn, Public Domain.

Chapter Ten: ORIGEN AND JUSTINIAN

1. Sources now unknown.

2. R. G. Bone, Justinian I, *The World Book Encyclopedia*, (1966), Volume XI, p. 168.
3. Charles F. Pfeiffer, *The Dead Sea Scrolls and the Bible*, (Grand Rapids, MI: Baker Book House, 1969).

Chapter Eleven:
ELIJAH AND JOHN THE BAPTIST/ JACOB AND ESAU

1. C. I. Scofield, *The New Scofield Reference Bible*, p. 1022.
2. Matthew Henry, *Commentary on the Whole Bible*, (Marshallton, DE: Sovereign Grace Publishers, 1972), Volume II, N.T. p. 971.

Chapter Twelve: REMEMBERED LIVES/ DEJA VU, DEMONS

1. Ian Stevenson, M.D., *Twenty Cases Suggestive of Reincarnation*, (Richmond: University Press of Virginia, 1980).
2. Merrill F. Unger, ThD., PhD., *Demons in the World Today*, (Wheaton, IL: Tyndale House, 1971) pgs. 8-13.
3. Ibid., pgs. 113-114.
4. Pat Brooks, *Out: In the Name of Jesus*, (Carol Stream, IL: Creation House, 1972).
5. Ian Stevenson, *Twenty Cases.*
6. Kurt Koch, ThD., *Occult Bondage and Deliverance*, (Grand Rapids, MI: Kregel Publications, 1972).
7. C. I. Scofield, *The New Scofield Reference Bible*, p. 1003.
8. Don Basham, *Can A Christian Have A Demon?*, (Monroeville, PA: Whitaker Books, 1971).
9. Kurt Koch, ThD., *Occult Bondage and Deliverance*, pgs. 67-71. See also Barry Wood, *Questions New Christians Ask*, pg. 686.
10. Hal Lindsey (With C. C. Carlson), *Satan is Alive and Well on Planet Earth*, (Grand Rapids, MI: Zondervan, 1972), pgs. 159-161.
11. Merrill F. Unger, *Demons in the World Today*, p. 185.

12. Ibid., p. 185.
13. Jessie Penn-Lewis, *The Spiritual Warfare*, (Fort Washington, PA: The Christian Literature Crusade, 1962), p. 21.
14. United Press International, (News - Journal Papers, Wilmington, DE, January 29, 1975).
15. Hal Lindsey, *Satan is Alive and Well on Planet Earth*, pgs. 164-165.
16. Merrill F. Unger, *Demons in the World Today*, pgs. 190-203.
17. Pat Robertson, *Answers to 200 of Life's Most Probing Questions*, (Nashville, TN: Thomas Nelson, 1984), pgs. 121-123.
18. C. S. Lewis, *The Best of C. S. Lewis, The Screwtape Letters*, (NY: The MacMillan Co., Christianity Today Edition, 1969), preface, p. 13.

Chapter Thirteen: SATAN, WITCHCRAFT

1. Pat Robertson, *Answers to 200 of Life's Most Probing Questions*, pgs. 48-49.
2. Hal Lindsey, *Satan is Alive and Well on Planet Earth*, p. 74.
3. J. Stafford Wright, *Christianity and the Occult*, (Chicago: Moody Press, 1972).
4. Merrill F. Unger, *Demons in the World Today*, pgs. 17-18.
5. Ibid., p. 57.
6. Hal Lindsey, *Satan is Alive and Well on Planet Earth*, pgs. 207-228.
7. Ibid., pgs. 133,134,158,159.
8. Ibid.
9. Ibid., pgs. 207-228.
10. C. S. Lovett, *Dealing with the Devil*, (Baldwin Park, CA: Personal Christianity, 1967).
11. Kurt Koch, ThD., *Occult Bondage and Deliverance*, pgs. 85-130.

Recommended Reading on Lucifer worship:

* Jack Harris, *Freemasonry,: The Invisible Cult in our Midst*,

(Chattanooga, TN: Global Publishers, 1983).
* Roy Livesey, *Understanding the New Age*, (Chichester, England: New Wine Press, 1986). Distributed in America by Destiny Image, P. O. Box 351, Shippensburg, PA, 17257.
* Ed Decker and Dave Hunt, *The God Makers: A Shocking Expose of What the Mormon Church Really Believes*, (Eugene, OR: Harvest House, 1984).

Chapter Fourteen: EDGAR CAYCE

1. Jess Stearn, *Edgar Cayce, The Sleeping Prophet*, (Garden City, NY: Doubleday, 1966).
2. Some early sources now unknown.
3. Joseph Millard, *Edgar Cayce, Mystery Man of Miracles*, quoted by Gordon Lindsay, *Sorcery in America Series*, Volume II, pgs. 17-27, (Dallas: Christ for the Nations, 1973).
4. Jess Stearn, *Edgar Cayce, The Sleeping Prophet*, p. 10.
5. Jeffrey Furst, *Edgar Cayce's Story of Jesus*, (NY: Coward-McCann, 1968), Twelfth Printing, 1986, p. 81.
6. Ibid., pgs. 73 76, 77.
7. Ibid., pgs. 23, 31, 39, 81.
8. Ibid., p. 81.
9. Ibid., p. 76.
10. Ibid., pgs. 80, 81.
11. Ibid., p. 81.
12. Ibid., p. 81.

Chapter Fifteen: MORE CAYCE

1. Jeffrey Furst, *Edgar Cayce's Story of Jesus*, p. 51.
2. Bart J. Bok, *Astrology*, The World Book Encyclopedia, (1966), Volume I, p. 784a.
3. Mary Ellen Carter, *My Years with Edgar Cayce, The Personal Story of Gladys Davis Turner*, (NY: Harper & Row, 1972), p. 63. Also Jeffrey Furst, *Edgar Cayce's Story of Jesus*, pgs. 342-346.

4. Josh McDowell and Don Stewart, *Understanding the Occult, Handbook of Today's Religions,* (San Bernadino, CA: Here's Life Publishers, 1982), pgs. 37-45.
5. Jeffrey Furst, *Edgar Cayce's Story of Jesus*, pgs. 77, 78.
6. C. I. Scofield, *The New Scofield Reference Bible*, p. 1351.
7. Jeffrey Furst, *The Return of Frances Willard,* (NY: Coward-McCann & Geoghegan, 1971), p. 152.
8. Jeffrey Furst, *Edgar Cayce's Story of Jesus*, p. 29.
9. Ibid., p. 28.
10. Ibid., p. 144.
11. Robert A. Morey, *Reincarnation and Christianity*, (Minneapolis: Bethany House, 1980), p. 27.
12. Texe Marrs, *Dark Secrets of the New Age,* (Westchester, IL: Crossway Books, 1987), p. 258.
13. Gordon Lindsay, *Sorcery in America* Series, Volume II (Dallas: Christ for the Nations, 1973), p. 20.
14. Ibid., p. 20.

Chapter Sixteen:

HUMAN REASONING - RUTH MONTGOMERY

1. Jeanne Dixon, *Reincarnation and Prayers to Live By*, (NY: William Morrow, 1970).
2. See also Josh McDowell and Don Stewart, *Understanding the Occult*, pgs. 55-61; Hal Lindsey, *Satan is Alive and Well on Planet Earth*, pgs. 114-128.
3. Ruth Montgomery, *Here and Hereafter*, (NY: Coward McCann, 1968), pgs. 223-224.
4. James Kennedy, *Evangelism Explosion*, (Wheaton, IL: Tyndale House, 1970), Edition 3, p. 45.

Chapter Seventeen:

MORE HUMAN REASONING - HEAD AND CRANSTON

1. Joseph Head and S. L. Cranston, *Reincarnation, An East-West*

Anthology, (Wheaton, IL: Theosophical Publishing House, 1981).

2. Ibid., p. 25.
3. Ibid., p. 25.
4. Ibid., p. 25.
5. Ibid., p. 26.
6. This statement appeared in a 1961 edition, not found in 1981 copy.
7. Head and Cranston, *Reincarnation, An East-West Anthology*, p. 32.
8. Ibid., p. 33.
9. Ibid., p. 34.

Chapter Eighteen: THEOSOPHY

1. William C. Irvine, Ed., *Heresies Exposed*, (Neptune, NJ: Loizaux Brothers, 1985), Thirty-Ninth Printing, A. McD. Redwood, "Theosophy", pgs. 187-192.
2. C. S. Lewis, *Mere Christianity*, (NY: The MacMillan Co., 1952), Edition 41, p. 56.
3. John Phillips, *The Voice of Prophecy*, (Chicago, IL: Moody Press, 1969).
4. Mrs. Annie Besant, quoted in *Heresies Exposed*, p. 189.
5. Dr. Graham Scroggie, quoted in *Heresies Exposed*, p. 192.
6. James R. Adair and Ted Miller, Editors, *We found our Way Out*, (Grand Rapids: Chapter 13, as told to Don Mainprize.)
7. For more on Madame Blavatsky and Theosophy, See Constance Cumbey, *The Hidden Dangers of the Rainbow*, (Shreveport, LA: Huntington House, 1983), pgs. 44-53, and Walter Martin, *The Kingdom of the Cults*, (Minneapolis: Bethany House, 36th Printing, 1985), chapter "Theosophy," pgs. 246-260. Also, Dave Hunt, *Peace, Prosperity and the Coming Holocaust*, (Eugene, OR: Harvest House, 1983), pgs. 123-127.

Chapter Nineteen: SHIRLEY MacLAINE AND COMPANY

1. Lytle W. Robinson, *Is It True What They Say About Edgar Cayce?*, (Seattle, WA: Vulcan Books, 1980), p. 46.
2. F. Lagard Smith, *Out On a Broken Limb*, (Eugene, OR: Harvest House, 1986), p. 164.
3. Gary DeMar, *The New Age Movement: A Fear of Shadows*, (in the Biblical Worldview, Volume 3, Number 9), Sept. 1987.
4. Texe Marrs, *Dark Secrets of the New Age*, (Westchester, IL: Crossway Books, 1987), pgs. 229-247.
5. Dave Hunt, *Peace, Prosperity and the Coming Holocaust*, pgs. 74-83.
6. Donald E. Wildmon, National Federation for Decency, Tupelo, MS, (in a letter to supporters, Aug. 1987).

Chapter Twenty: RAINBOWS AND SWASTIKAS

1. Texe Marrs, *Dark Secrets of the New Age*, pgs. 15-17.
2. Ibid., pgs. 63, 136-151.
3. Constance Cumbey, *The Hidden Dangers of the Rainbow*, pgs. 78, 83, 142, 143.
4. Dave Hunt, *Peace, Prosperity and the Coming Holocaust*, pgs. 209-211.
5. Texe Marrs, *Dark Secrets of the New Age*, pgs. 136-151, 162-165.
6. Ibid., back cover.
7. Diane Salvatore, Page-Up Service (News-Journal Papers, Wilmington, DE, August 22, 1987).
8. Texe Marrs, Dark Secrets of the New Age, pgs. 19, 56-61.
9. Constance Cumbey, *The Hidden Dangers of the Rainbow*, pgs. 19-25, 68, 69, 73, 81-83.
10. Ibid., back cover, showing ad published world-wide by the Tara Center, NY, April 25, 1982.
11. Ibid.
12. Ibid., p. 67.

13. Texe Marrs, *Dark Secrets of the New Age*, pgs. 60, 138, 139.
14. Constance Cumbey, *The Hidden Dangers of the Rainbow*, pgs. 19-25.
15. Ibid., pgs. 29-30, 54-71.
16. Ibid., p. 66
17. Ibid., p. 102-110.
18. Texe Marrs, *Dark Secrets of the New Age*, pgs. 119-135.
19. Constance Cumbey, pgs. 79, 91, 92, 99-120.
20. Jean Michel Angebert, *The Occult and the Third Reich*, (NY: MacMillan, 1974).
21. Constance Cumbey, *The Hidden Dangers of the Rainbow*, pgs. 69, 107-120.
22. Dave Hunt, *Peace, Prosperity and the Coming Holocaust*, pgs. 129-143.
23. Ibid., pg 220: Constance Cumbey, *The Hidden Dangers of the Rainbow*, pgs 82, 83, 118, 143: Texe Marrs, *Dark Secrets of the New Age*, pgs. 136-151.
24. Texe Marrs, *Dark Secrets of the New Age*, p. 74, p. 273 note for Chapter 7:1. See also Jack Harris, *Freemasonry: The Invisible Cult in Our Midst*, (Chattanooga, TN: Global Publishers, 1983).
25. Texe Marrs, *Dark Secrets of the New Age*, pgs. 24-34.
26. Dave Hunt, *Peace, Prosperity and the Coming Holocaust*, p. 210.
27. John White, in the introduction to the 1979 International Cooperation Council Directory (now known as the Unity-In-Diversity Council), quoted by Constance Cumbey, *Hidden Dangers of the Rainbow*, pgs. 111-112.
28. Webster's Seventh New Collegiate Dictionary (Chicago: Merriam Co., 1965), p. 572.
29. Texe Marrs, *Dark Secrets of the New Age*, p. 126.
30. Dave Hunt, *Peace, Prosperity and the Coming Holocaust*, especially pgs. 187-203.

31. Ibid., pgs. 224-232.

Recommended Reading:

* The books used in this chapter by Cumbey, Hunt and Marrs, referenced above.
* Roy Livesey, *Understanding the New Age*, (Chichester, England: New Wine Press, 1986), distributed in America by Destiny Image, P. O. Box 351, Shippensburg, PA, 17257.
* Douglas R. Groothuis, *The New Age Movement* (Downers Grove IL: Inter-Varisty Press, 1986).
* Must reading for those concerned: Marlin Maddoux, *America Betrayed!*, (Shreveport, LA: Huntington House, 1984). Schools and Children; Ibid., pgs. 50-73. Humanist Manifesto and Humanism, Ibid., pgs. 17-22.

Chapter Twenty-One:

PERSONAL TESTIMONY - THE WAY OUT

Recommended Reading:

* The New Testament
* David C. Needham, *Birthright: Christian, Do You Know Who You Are?*, (Portland, OR: Multnomah Press, 1979).
* Pat Robertson, *Answers to 200 of Life's Most Probing Questions*, (Nashville, TN: Thomas Nelson, 1984).
* J. I. Packer, *I Want to be a Christian*, (Wheaton, IL: Tyndale House, 1977).
* Hannah Whitall Smith, *The Christian's Secret of a Happy Life*, (Old Tappan, NJ: Fleming H. Revell, 30th printing, 1979).

DEAR FUTURE READER:

You've found this old book. There is one world government, one world religion, under one strong leader. You remember the "Quantum Leap," when so many Christians suddenly disappeared, but you made it somehow and things now are very different. Many people will see what has really happened and call on Jesus Christ. I pray that you will be one of them. It won't be easy for you, but it's not too late. The Bible, not the New Age one, but the real one says:

> And I saw the thrones, and they sat upon them, and judgment was given unto them; and I saw the souls of them that were beheaded for the witness of Jesus, and for the word of God, and who had not worshipped the beast, neither his image, neither had received his mark upon their foreheads, or in their hands; and they lived and reigned with Christ a thousand years (Revelation 20:4).

Jesus Christ will come back to earth very soon; the beast will only reign for seven years altogether. Through Jesus Christ, you can still find eternal life. God the Father, the Creator of all things loves you and wants to set you free.